THE

GLASS

COMPANY

HOW TO LEAD, HIRE, AND SELL
IN THE TRANSPARENT WORLD

By William Paolillo

Published in the United States by
Insight Publishing Company
Copyright 2015
707 West Main Street, Suite 5
Sevierville, TN 37862
800-987-7771
www.insightpublishing.com
Cover by Steve Wilson
Formatting by Chris Ott

ISBN 978-1-62452-120-1

10 9 8 7 6 5 4 3 2 1

Table of Contents

Foreword

The research is clear and compelling: companies that do good for society, do well in business—better than the competition. Their successful business growth is a result of being *transparent*. *To be transparent is to expose our core beliefs and values for scrutiny by our stakeholders.* So why would we lift the proverbial kimono? If you do not do it, someone will do it for you.

Your story is no longer your story. Your employees, customers, and suppliers are telling your story, where their comments are recorded on the Internet forever. The business world is now an open book, including the way you conduct business with your suppliers, and your costs, the salaries of your employees, as well as how you treat your employees and customers.

To navigate your way in a transparent world, we are required to change our perspectives and the assumptions we've been led to believe as truths. We need to align our values and the values of our business with values of our employees, customers, and society. Once we understand whom we want on the team, we then need to co-create a common vision. This is the disruptive nature of transparency: controlling *with* versus *controlling over* your employees, suppliers, and customers. They will share your message with the world on the Internet.

The Glass Company has assembled a collection of experts who will help you understand what is required for you and your company to leverage the disruptive nature of transparency.

Dedication

To Michael, Gabrielle, Isabelle, and James – Love You.
Those who do good, do well... Dream Big.

Acknowledgements

Thank you to the contributing authors for their collaboration and control with::Ed, Chuck, Joe, Deb, Solange, Dave, & Andy.

Thank you to the Case Western Reserve Doctorate of Management Cohort 2015 and our professors – SISU.

Chapter 1
Flourishing Business in a Transparent World
with Dr. Edward Straub

> A PEACOCK spreading its gorgeous tail mocked a crane that
> passed by, ridiculing the ashen hue of its plumage and saying, "I am
> robed like a king, in gold and purple and all the colors of the rainbow;
> while you have not a bit of color on your wings."
>
> "True," replied the crane, "but I soar to the heights of heaven and
> lift up my voice to the stars, while you walk below, like a cock, among
> the birds of the dunghill."
>
> —*Aesop's Fables*

The moral of this fable is that to be successful at things that really matter; it takes more than appearances—there must be substance.

Today, in the transparent world powered by the worldwide web you no longer control your story. Your story is created and recreated every day through interactions with your employees, customers, and suppliers; comments posted to our company's message board, a blog, a website, or social media. How do we navigate this complex world and ensure that our stakeholders really understand our company and our company's message? How do we reconcile this new reality with traditional business dogma focused on control and relative advantage? If our message is not our own, what do we tell our employees and customers? How do we succeed?

The Glass Company provides insight into the new transparent world of business—an environment reflective of challenges and opportunities for revenue and professional growth. Investors, current and potential employees, suppliers, clients, and potential clients continually assess whether—and, if so, how much—to invest their resources in your enterprise. So whether they see your Transparent World in a positive light or their view includes some not so positive and even some negatives realities, transparency is essential to growth. Throughout this book the contributing authors and I make it crystal clear that transparency is the key to attracting resources needed for corporate, employee, client, and investor growth and success.

The research is clear and compelling: companies that do good for society do well in business—better than the competition. Their successful business growth is a result of being *transparent*. One of the benefits includes growth from customer, employee, and supplier referrals. Companies that do well and excel, recognize that in the transparent business world, stakeholders are more than targets to bombard with messages—they are bridges for their messages and a means for broader dissemination enabled by the Internet. *The Glass Company* navigates the way.

To navigate our way in a transparent world, we are required to change our perspectives and the assumptions we've been led to believe as truths. In short, we don't strive to succeed. We strive to *flourish*. Flourishing involves aligning our values and the values of our business with the values our customers and society hold dear. We clarify our vision for our company and share this with the world. We become transparent.

"But isn't business about the bottom line—cutting costs and increasing revenue?" you ask. "Shouldn't I create an image that I think is in demand and feed that to my target demographic?" That's just it. Organizing your business around the principles based on the concepts of flourishing, sharing control, and being transparent *is* a source of advantage. But it also runs counter to many of the industrial-age assumptions that have come to be mistaken for absolute truths. Being transparent is letting go of our desire to control every aspect of our message and engaging in a process of co-creation with our employees and customers.

To *flourish* is to have more than financial success. Flourishing adds the individual and social dimensions of human well-being and the well-established concept of sustainability. At its core flourishing is a function of *connectedness* and *meaning* between people [Reference 1]. We can think of these heady subjects as being transparent in our business, transparent in our motives with the community, transparent in how we treat our employees, transparent in how we conduct business with suppliers, and transparent in how we interact with our customers. To be transparent is to expose our core beliefs and values for scrutiny by our stakeholders.

In the transparent world we are compelled to give up the idea of dictating our company's message in favor of co-creating it with our stakeholders. The 2014 BSR/Globescan "State of Sustainable Business Survey" identified transparency as "the most effective way to improve low public trust in business" and one of three [Ref. 2] "mega-trends that will have the most impact on business over the next twenty-four months" [Ref. 2]. The focus of this book is transparency as a driver within a flourishing business. The focus of this chapter is to introduce you to some of the key concepts behind a transparent, flourishing company. We will also, very briefly, touch on some of the support for these concepts compiled from a mix of decades of business experience from the C-suite and the consultant's chair as well as original academic research and a survey of the literature.

Being connected and creating meaning with others is to be transparent in business. Connectedness is the recognition that relationships exist between and across individuals, teams, organizations, and the environment. Meaning is having purpose, beginning with a sense of self-awareness and extending to a broader sense of purposeful action and effective outcomes. Finding meaning in work and business grows from an alignment of work with our values. Businesses, organizations, and project teams can capitalize on this alignment. Looking inwardly at our business, individual employees are more engaged and generally produce better output when their values align with the organization[Ref. 3]. To flourish, however, is to go beyond value alignment. For businesses to flourish, employees and the organization must have a sense of *wholeness* [Ref. 3-4]. This wholeness extends outwardly to customers. With wholeness, individuals feel secure in their ability to express their thoughts freely and bring the entirety of their mental, physical, and emotional resources to bear.

For individuals to bring their whole self to a task, each must find it meaningful (1) and interact with others with whom each individual feels connected. Connection, meaning, and wholeness liberate organizational innovation, engagement, and productivity. When this happens, previously intractable problems are resolved often creating new markets, business models, and industries in the [Ref. 3-4]. Employees engaged in work they believe to be meaningful are intrinsically motivated to complete a task and complete it well, reducing the need for managers to devise various carrots and sticks and continuously monitor their activity [Ref. 5].

But just how do we align values and make this connection? More to the point, how do we communicate with our employees to let them know this is a priority? Communication is a well-known and well-studied area of business and management research [Ref. 6-8]. We're not going to talk about communicating or crafting sticky messages. That stuff is important. Got it. But beyond the number of syllables in a catch-phrase or the colors in a logo, what is less well publicized is how the substance behind *what* is communicated resonates with people and why. The context, the media, and the manner in which people send and receive messages all have meaning. Understanding what, when, where, and how to communicate a meaningful message are characteristics of emotional intelligence (EQ) [Ref. 9].

EQ is a popular concept and is becoming more generally accepted in practice and theory, as supporting evidence continues to build [Ref. 10-12]. EQ is "the capacity for recognizing our own feelings and those of others, for motivating ourselves, and for managing emotions in ourselves and in our relationships" [Ref. 13 p. 317]. It was first described in 1990 by Salovey and Mayer but exploded into the mainstream academic and practitioner consciousness in 1995 when Daniel Goleman published his book melding the theory of EQ with his previous research on leadership and high-performing individuals [Ref. 14].

Emotional Intelligence can be summarized in four dimensions: Two, individually-oriented and two, socially-oriented. The two *individual* dimensions are 1) self-awareness, being able to recognize one's own emotions as they occur, and 2) empathy, being able to recognize emotions in others as they occur.

The social *dimensions* of EQ are 1) social awareness, being able to manage one's emotions, and 2) relationship management, which is the ability to manage emotions in others [Ref. 4 & 14]. The two social dimensions of EQ are further described by Goleman [Ref. 9 pg. 11] as Social Intelligence (SQ), which is "acting wisely in human relations." SQ builds on the social awareness element of EQ and adds to it something Goleman calls "social facility" or the ability to "smoothly" interact with others through synchrony, self-presentation, influence, and concern [Ref. 9 pg. 83].

A difference between average leaders and successful, emotionally intelligent leaders is that the latter can effectively apply the right tool to the right situation. They know that context matters and what works in one situation may not work in another. Playfulness is one of these tools. Playfulness involves a willingness to experiment and suspend rules and to approach tasks "in an imaginative, non-serious, or metaphoric manner so as to enhance intrinsic enjoyment, involvement, and satisfaction. Emotional intelligence, specifically empathy and self-awareness, are what effective leaders use to create connections between people [Ref. 4]. Emotional and social intelligence can lead to better relationships—between leaders and followers and with customers and customer groups—improved ability to address and resolve conflict, enhanced communication, and improved outcomes [Ref. 2,9,14, and 15].

A meaningful, connected relationship with one's employees, teammates, and customers requires continual effort [Ref. 16]. Constant, thoughtful communication requires consistently making sense of observations in order to share them with other team members and help them make sense of the information. This sense-making effort can be thought of as dialectic, or engaging in a back-and-forth conversation with others, exposing and discussing the merits *and faults* of each relative position openly and in context. This conscious comparison results in open, mindful behavior and decisions [Ref. 17].

People are less likely to act (or post) rashly or in an emotionally-charged fit when they are acting mindfully. The idea of "mindfulness" is an old one, originating in Eastern religion in about the fourth or third centuries BCE [Ref. 4 & 18].

> Mindfulness . . . is as much about what people do with what they notice as it is about the activity of noticing itself . . . It is the enlarged set of possibilities that suggests unexpected deviation that needs to be corrected and new sources of ignorance that become new imperatives for noticing.
>
> —*Weick, Sutcliffe, and Obstfeld*

If an organization or team is going to be mindful, its employees must be engaged. People engaged in their work tend to find it interesting [Ref. 19]. For individuals, to be engaged is to concurrently be in a prolonged mentally and emotionally "positive, fulfilling, work-related state ... characterized by vigor, dedication, and absorption" [Ref. 19 pg. 74]. This creates a virtuous circle and flourishing environment in which motivation, dedication, and satisfaction can lead to improved performance and even improved individual health, probably as a result of reduced stress [Ref. 5 & 20]. In 2002, Gallup estimated that disengaged workers cost the US economy about $350B [Ref. 21]. By 2013, Gallup's estimate of the cost of disengaged workers had risen to between $450-$550B [Ref. 22].

In a 2015 survey of 350 business owners [Ref. 2], 38 percent self-identified as having a company built around making positive contributions. These business owners are three to four times more likely to have also rated their personal *and company* visions as purposeful.

The fact that this is how business owners view themselves and their business is important. These businesses are organized by their leaders to do well in society and, as a result, they do well. Nearly half of these businesses also view themselves as fixtures in their communities, compared to only 16 percent of those businesses who identify less strongly with their contribution to society.

We know that the stronger the bond of individuals within a group, the more likely they are to share information, trust, and attitudes [Ref. 23]. These are the bonds of community. Today, communities exist in more than a traditional geographic sense. Virtual communities have given new strength to so-called "weak ties" act as bridges [Ref. 24], connecting less familiar social groups, and broadening access to information easily for both the group seeking it and the group intending to transfer it [Ref. 25]. But what is the message?

Through co-creation, companies align the values of their leadership team, employees, and important stakeholders to create a shared vision. Shared vision is a critical element of relationship quality and essential for individual engagement and team functioning [Ref. 26 & 27-4]. A shared vision happens when a common desired future state exists among a group of individuals, the individuals have hope that it can be achieved, and share enough identity to relate to it [Ref. 26 & 28].

If these concepts seem like the idealistic delusions of Millennials sitting in their parents' spare bedroom, milking their insurance while they wait for their killer app to hit it big, think again. Half of the business owners responding to our survey have been in business for more than twenty years. These concepts are sustainable for the long-term. To think about business in terms of aligned values, "correctness," meaning, and shared vision is to think differently.

Business schools teach and consultants sell the ideas that we succeed by gaining relative advantage over our competition. We identify a niche in the market or a weakness in a competitor. Maybe we find a low-cost supplier and outsource production. In the pursuit of this, we typically use sayings like "battling for market share" or "getting dirty in the trenches" or "hitting a home run." These metaphors, associated with warfare and sports, prime our thought patterns and predispose us to short-term objectives [Ref. 29]. People use metaphors to understand complex topics or issues. Metaphors help us to create mental models in unfamiliar or complicated situations through the use of familiar phrases, relationships, and tasks. When we do this, metaphors "bring forth semantic, behavioral, and affective responses...characteristic of the source domain' [Ref. 30 pg. 276].

Therefore, we must be mindful of the metaphors we use when we describe our teams, our business, and our work environment. Sports and military metaphors have been shown to elicit a sense of limited, mission-oriented objectives. Family and community metaphors generally imply broad, cross-functional objectives, teamwork, nurturing, and support [Ref. 30].

Leaders who think differently change the message they send by changing the metaphors they use and the images they evoke. Creating community and having a positive effect on society are long-term objectives, but ones that are becoming more generally acknowledged as key determinants of successful and sustainable business [Ref. 4] and transparency in business, and are seen as the number one way to increase public trust [Ref. 2].

According to the 2014 "State of Sustainable Business" survey, businesses in the United States have significantly more room for improvement in this area than those outside North America [Ref. 2]. This signals an area of opportunity for today's business leader. In our survey, 75 percent of the business owners who identified their business as positively contributing to society also described themselves as "results-" or "profit-oriented." These are not leaders in business to give away product—they are in business to make money, but also envision making the world a better place while doing it. The two goals are not incompatible and our data tells us that they will be more effective through transparency and co-creation; in short, by becoming a flourishing company.

In many industries, work teams are the primary means for getting work done [Ref. 31]. Research suggests that the effectiveness of our employee teams should be considered as more than a measure of the quantitative output produced by the team. Sure results matter, but effectiveness should also include *viability*, which speaks to a team's ability to continue performing work [Ref. 32]. Key factors contributing to team viability include individual satisfaction and elements such as: a willingness to continue working together, cohesion, and unsurprisingly, communication [Ref. 32]. But these factors do not stand on their own—the context matters. Sharing the leader's vision and values, and the vision for the company, helps to create a flourishing environment within the organization [Ref. 33].

Sixty one percent of the business leaders in our survey attributed their success to making human connections ahead of setting goals and accomplishing tasks. This is for the entire population, spanning businesses that strongly claim their purpose is rooted around a positive contribution to society to those who stake their claim somewhere south of world improvement. The bottom line with this statistic is that business owners, regardless of their aspirations, recognize the value of connecting with people— employees, shareholders, suppliers, or customers. Business leaders who strongly identify their business with creating societal value also claim to listen more closely to their stakeholders.

When we interact with our customers online we give up control of our company's message. Through openness, we create connection and meaning with our customers. They take the message, they share it and it grows. We cannot expect our message to be parroted word-for-word because it is no longer our own. There will be changes and we need to be okay with them because the objectives are aligned; they involve a net positive benefit for society. That is the point! If we're honest and open in this regard and if we share our vision and values with our customers in the transparent world, we will flourish.

Chapter 2
Leadership in a Transparent World
with Chuck Sarka

I first read this story in the inaugural edition of *Chicken Soup, for the Soul* by Jack Canfield and Mark Victor Hansen. Since then have seen it posted at various times on Facebook and other media venues. The story took place back in 1978 in Phoenix, Arizona, between a young child and a very special fireman, and is attributed to the first wish for the Make-a-Wish foundation. It grabbed my heartstrings then just as it will grab yours now thirty-eight years later. Why? Because it is not just a story about the overwhelming empathy and courage of Fireman Bob and the strength of a little boy fighting a terminal disease, but because it is a leadership lesson that will stand the test of time.

The twenty-six-year-old mother stared down at her son who was dying of terminal leukemia. Although her heart was filled with sadness, she also had a strong feeling of determination. Like any parent she wanted her son to grow up and fulfill all his dreams. Now that was no longer possible; the leukemia would see to that. But she still wanted her son's dreams to come true.

She took her son's hand and asked, "Bopsy, did you ever think about what you wanted to be once you grew up? Did you ever dream and wish what you would do with your life?"

"Mommy," he replied, "I always wanted to be a fireman when I grew up."

Mom smiled back and said, "Let's see if we can make your wish come true."

Later that day she went to her local fire department in Phoenix, Arizona, where she met Fireman Bob, who had a heart as big as Phoenix. She explained her son's final wish and asked if it might be possible to give her six-year-old son a ride around the block on a fire engine.

Fireman Bob said, "Look, we can do better than that. If you'll have your son ready at seven o'clock Wednesday morning, we'll make him an honorary fireman for the whole day. He can come down to the fire station, eat with us, go out on all the fire calls—the whole nine yards! And if you'll give us his sizes, we'll get a real fire uniform for him, with a real fire hat—not a toy one—with the emblem of the Phoenix Fire Department on it, a yellow slicker like we wear, and rubber boots. They're all manufactured right here in Phoenix, so we can get them fast."

Three days later Fireman Bob picked up Bopsy, dressed him in his fire uniform, and escorted him from his hospital bed to the waiting hook-and-ladder truck. Bopsy got to sit on the back of the truck and help steer it back to the fire station. He was in heaven. There were three fire calls in Phoenix that day and Bopsy got to go out on all three calls.

He rode in the different fire engines, the paramedic's van, and even the fire chief's car. He was also videotaped for a local news program.

Having his dream come true, with all the love and attention lavished upon him, so deeply touched Bopsy that he lived three months longer than any doctor thought possible.

One night all of his vital signs began to drop dramatically and the head nurse, who believed in the hospice concept that no one should die alone, began to call the family members to the hospital. Then she remembered the day Bopsy had spent as a fireman, so she called the Fire Chief and asked if it would be possible to send a fireman in uniform to the hospital to be with Bopsy as he made his transition.

The chief replied, "We can do better than that. We'll be there in five minutes. Will you please do me a favor? When you hear the sirens screaming and see the lights flashing, will you announce over the PA system that there is not a fire? It's just the fire department coming to see one of its finest members one more time. And will you open the window to his room?"

About five minutes later a hook and ladder truck arrived at the hospital, extended its ladder up to Bopsy's third floor open window and five firefighters climbed up the ladder into Bopsy's room. With his mother's permission, they hugged him and held him and told him how much they loved him.

With his dying breath, Bopsy looked up at the fire chief and said, "Chief, am I really a fireman now?"

"Yes, Bopsy, you are a fireman now," the chief said. With those words, Bopsy smiled and closed his eyes one last time. He passed away later that evening.

> The currency for the transparent world is a positive moment of connection, stored as an online post or remembered moment by a customer, supplier, and employee.

Each and every person who interacts with your company has individual hopes and dreams. Each person on your team has internal struggles, not as dire as Bopsy's but still important to them. Your customers, employees, and suppliers still have points of pain that are real to them and at times debilitating. What if each time your followers came to you with a problem, question, or suggestion and, instead of putting them off to take the next phone call, run to the next meeting, answer that next e-mail, you paused, listened to them and then said "I can do better than that."

Leadership in the transparent world is problematic for people and business leaders who believe that what has worked in the past will continue to work in the future. The Internet has changed the playing field, and in more ways than simply accelerating the pace of business. People who post reviews or make comments on the Internet have a propensity to be lovers or haters, and the person making the post may not even be qualified to create the post. Leaders/owners no longer control their companies' messages. Your story is no longer your story.

The prescription of how to lead is something that changes based upon the times. In the industrial age, leadership reflected the machines that created value and was based upon command and control—you controlled machines. In the Industrial era, people were viewed as parts of machines—we controlled their behavior with a defined process and got a predictable output.

In the knowledge economy, *people and their relationships* are the means of production. To unleash the true potential of business, we need to control *with* as opposed to control *over* (Boland 79). The role of the leader has changed—it is now to co-create a common vision and facilitate positive connection during a company's interactions with the transparent world. A leader's ability to facilitate co-creation and generate positive interactions among suppliers, employees, and customers—as they self-organize around the chaos of your business—is what creates a growing, thriving company in the transparent world. These positive points of interaction serve as currency, chips in the bank, to build your business in the good times and defend your company when under attack.

So how do we create chips in the bank and what does a chip in the bank look like in the transparent world?

We co-create with our suppliers, customers, and employees, recognizing them as not an end for our message but as a means of broad dissemination on the Internet. To co-create with individuals, we need to understand where they are coming from—their Terminal Values. The currency for the transparent world is a positive moment of connection, stored as an online post or a remembered moment by a customer, supplier, or employee. These accumulated moments of positivity are chips in the bank.

Terminal Values

We have identified common characteristics of successful, transparent companies. They strongly agree that they pursue win-win relationships with customers, employees, and other key stakeholders. They also win by emphasizing human connections and relationships versus setting goals and accomplishing tasks. A key to a transparent company's success is that they lead using Terminal values versus Instrumental values.

TERMINAL VALUE	DEFINITION
Achievement	Successful completion of visible tasks or projects
Advancement	Opportunity to get ahead, ambition, aspiring to higher levels
Adventure	Challenge, risk taking, testing limits
Aesthetics	Desire for beauty, artistic
Appearance	Looking good, dressing well, keeping fit
Authority	Having the power to direct events, make things happen
Belonging	Being connected to and liked by others
Challenge	Testing intellectual or physical limits
Communication	Open dialogue, exchange of views
Community	Actively involved and contributing to the community
Competence	Being good at what we do, capable, effective
Competition	Winning, doing better than others
Consensus	Making decisions everyone can live with
Courage	To stand up for our beliefs
Creativity	Finding new ways to do things, innovative
Diplomacy	Finding common ground with difficult people and situations
Environment	Respecting the future of the Earth
Fairness	Similar opportunity for everyone
Family	Taking care and spending time with loved ones
Forgiveness	To pardon others
Friendship	Close companionship, ongoing relationships
Health	Maintain and enhance physical well being
Helping	Taking care of others, doing what they need
Honesty	Tell the truth with compassion
Inner Harmony	Freedom from inner conflict, integrated, whole
Integrity	Acting in line with beliefs
Intellectual Status	Being regarded as experts, persons who know
Intimacy	Emotional, spiritual connection
Knowledge	Seeking intellectual stimulation, new ideas, truth and understanding
Neatness	Tidy, orderly, clean
Peace	Constructive resolution of conflict
Perseverance	Pushing through to the end, completing the tasks
Personal Growth	Continual learning, development of new skills, self-awareness
Play	Fun, lightness, spontaneity
Pleasure	Personal satisfaction, enjoyment, delight
Power	Having control over other people
Prosperity	Flourishing, profitable, financially secure
Rationality	Consistent, logical, clear reasoning
Recognition	Noticing effective efforts
Respectful	Showing consideration, regarding with honor
Security	Freedom from worry, safe, risk free
Self-Acceptance	Building self-respect and self esteem
Self-Control	Self-disciplined, restrained
Spiritual Growth	Relationship to higher purpose, divine being
Stability	Certainty, predictability
Teamwork	Cooperating with others toward a common goal
Tolerance	To be respectful of others
Tradition	Respecting the way things have always been done

Terminal Values are five or six in number, are different at different points in our lives, but do not dramatically change throughout time. You will fight and die for your terminal values, you will quit your job if they are violated, and they are non-negotiable.

Some examples of Terminal values are Family, Integrity, Achievement, Competition, and Spirituality. You can access a diagnostic at glasscompanybook.com to understand your terminal values.

Instrumental values are a means to an end; they help you achieve your terminal values. They change, are negotiable, and people will be motivated by twenty-five at any one time. These are the values espoused in the Management by Objective school of management. Examples of instrumental values are money and a car. These instrumental values for my four children helped them achieve the terminal value of Pleasure—personal satisfaction, enjoyment, and delight.

What happens when you lead using terminal values versus instrumental values?

The Welty Building Company has grown from $30 million to more than $300 million dollars. Don Taylor, the owner and CEO, believes one the keys to the company's success is that Welty is the most emotionally intelligent building company—they listen.

Having emotionally intelligent delivery team members, or at least team members open to the idea of EQ, is a prerequisite for creating a commonly shared vision and common values across the many teams of contractors, subcontractors, users, designers, and suppliers, all participating in project delivery.

A typical construction project and jobsite can be characterized by testosterone-filled conversation and an attitude typified by commands like, "Just do your job. Follow the specifications and everything will work out." If it does not work out, the construction industry is one of the few places where customers and suppliers frequently sue each other.

In the recent building of a hospital wing for an addition to Akron Children's Hospital in Akron Ohio, Welty led the team that delivered the project for $178.5 million versus an original cost estimate of $240 million. So how did they do it? What we found in our interviews of the workforce at ACH was an example of emotionally intelligent leadership. The union workforce described working in a *"Blame-Free Environment," which meant that if something went wrong, the focus was on fixing the problem versus fixing blame. The workforce would recognize each other for a job well done by awarding each other a bambino sticker.* Awarding "bambinos" is akin to the Ohio State University football tradition of awarding buckeye stickers for a particularly good play and pasting them on their helmets. At the construction site, workers likewise proudly pasted these stickers on their hard hats.

So how did Welty become the most emotionally intelligent building company?

They interviewed and ultimately hired employees who exemplified the terminal values identified as key to the company's success—those reflecting emotional intelligence. The five terminal values for WBC are family, prosperity, teamwork, communication, and diplomacy, in that order. The terminal values for the WBC project managers and superintendents, the members leading the team at the construction site, in order, were family, prosperity, *diplomacy*, teamwork, and communication. Notice that diplomacy moved up to number three. WBC understood that to lead in the new transparent world of construction, they would need leaders on the jobsite who bring the team together and create positive moments of connection—chips in the bank.

When do we create a Chip in the Bank?

Years ago, when families where still allowed to venture to the gates at the airport to greet their loved ones, a consultant was sitting and waiting for his plane to arrive. As time passed a young mother with two cute, little twin girls came striding toward the gate.

The twins skipped just ahead of this young mother chanting, "Daddy is coming home on the big jet! Daddy is coming home on the big jet!"

Mom gently corralled them by the gate and within a short period of time the plane rolled up to the gate and passengers started to deplane. It wasn't long before the observant consultant pinpointed who their daddy was.

As dad walked off the plane the two little twins bolted toward him announcing to all in the gate area "Daddy is home!"

I ask you to pause for a moment before reading on and contemplate what this father said back to his daughters. Have your response? The fact is, he didn't say a word. He said *nothing*. He walked right by them. As he approached his wife, he asked if she had brought a raincoat.

Now, the first question one might ask is, "I wonder what this man does for a living?" I will even venture to say that if you told this father that you had a formula for ultimate success, he would quickly ask the price and reach for his wallet. The real irony is that he had been presented a golden moment to be great and he didn't even realize it. It went right over his head! You see, greatness isn't going to come to us cascading down like Niagara Falls. It is going to come a little drop at a time, by way of a little pat and a little praise.

Leadership success is achieved the same way. Depositing emotional chips in the hearts of your employees, suppliers, customers, and loved ones comes in little drops at a time. Be honest and ask yourself how many times you have pushed off a follower's request to meet, and you essentially "walked right by" him or her because there were more important things to do.

The customer's post is the new standard of product and service quality, and not simply defective-return data or evidence of a service failure. This online conversation is your golden moment as a leader to touch your employees, customers, and suppliers by putting building chips in the bank. A single online customer post about a specific store or general consumer website can influence millions of consumers.

The customer post is the ideal vehicle for creativity and innovation in a company. If you set your followers free they will grow and they will grow your business. The emergence of self-directed teams and a reliance on empowered workers greatly increases the importance of trust, as control mechanisms are reduced or removed and interaction increases. In the use of self-directed teams, trust must take the place of supervision because direct observation of employees becomes impractical. (Mayer, Davis, and Schoorman, 1998, p. 709)

In her book, *Love 2.0*, Barbara Fredrickson says the way for human beings to build chips in the bank, is by experiencing a positive moment of connection. *A mutual responsiveness based upon an interaction that you get me.* An example would be a nod or a smile during a face-to-face interaction. In the online environment this can be experienced by a quick response to a post about your product or service when you are having an issue and it is resolved (Paolillo 2013). Your ability to connect or have someone connect on your behalf for your company with an appropriate response of understanding and caring is what leadership is about in the transparent world. This positive moment of connection—a moment where I believe you understand me or we share in moment of happiness or sadness—leads to a release of the hormone oxytocin. Oxytocin, referred to as the "love hormone," promotes feelings of trust and empathy. This emotional contagion is an opportunity to build and broaden the relationship. Leaders must create positive account balances, draw them down when necessary, and be careful of running deficits.

Each of us has a head and a heart. From the head side of the equation we want to know why we are in a company, where they are going as a team, how we are doing—feedback—what's in it for us from a rewards standpoint and, if we have a problem, to whom can we turn for support. We want to know the rules of the game, however; we want to be lead from the heart. As the saying goes, "I don't care how much you know, until I know how much you care." We engage with leaders we believe in and who have built up emotional chips in our hearts.

How does a leader bank an emotional chip with his or her partners in business? The answer is that it depends. Each of us has our own language of appreciation, our own "feeling of being in" on things, and our own level of career meaning.

The first step is to connect with each of the suppliers, employees, and customers on a one-on-one basis. This can be done in the transparent world through the Internet by publically recognizing success and complaints. You need to consider treating everyone the same by treating them differently. Yes, you read that right. The old adage, "There is no I in team" is fundamentally flawed in a transparent world. Each of us has a different set of talents, thinking preferences, and behaviors that, when individually cultivated, grows into a dynamic team. Set them free and the team will tell your story and build your business.

Once a connection between you and your followers happens, you can then build credibility and trust, allowing for emotional chips to be deposited in another's heart. With a full emotional bank account, a leader can initiate change from a much stronger foundation. Leaders can ask for that extraordinary request but, more importantly, employees, suppliers, and customers who are emotionally connected to those leaders are engaged.

Leaders who have empty bank accounts with their followers are forced into an accounting term called a "death spiral" that often leads to disengagement or worse, a mass exodus. There is debated research that states "three times the praise for each oops." No matter what you believe, following the advice to do something and then "let the chips fall where they may" is a dangerous leadership strategy. Take care of your employees', suppliers,' and customers' emotional bank accounts and they, in turn, will take care of you.

Leadership needs to trust employees and customers with delivering the communication message. The moments of positivity that generate affirming moments of connection—chips in the bank—create extrinsic and intrinsic motivation for individuals to co-create with your company.

The question for leadership in a transparent world then becomes, "How do we create an environment that builds and broadens shared moments of positivity?"

Chapter 3
Centered Values: How to Align Your Company In the Transparent World
with Joe Mazzella

If you don't know where you are going, any road can take you there.
—Lewis Carroll

In today's transparent business world, just any road does not work. Both you and your employees need to know what road you have chosen, why and, most importantly, believe it is the right road.

Why is your chosen road so important? Not only do customers want quality products and services at a competitive price, they want immediate "response on demand." Our relationship with suppliers must be effective, so communication and collaboration are essential. We need to keep profits high and inventory low, so the syncopation of supply and demand must be orchestrated with precision to meet those objectives.

In order to achieve these imperatives, companies must retain talented employees, develop those with potential, and continue to attract new talent. The competitive edge for profitable, prosperous organizations is in establishing a coordinated effort, a clear vision, purpose, and direction. The cost of doing nothing is huge—customer walk-outs, inventory outages, low employee morale, and profit losses. Clients, suppliers, and senior management will show you the door. Essential employees and business partners will leave.

According to the Bureau of Labor Statistics, the median number of years that wage and salaried workers had been with their current employer was 4.6 years in January 2014. The day of passing out thirty-five-plus years' service awards is over. The battle for talent has become one of the hottest contests within the business world. Who will win? The winners will be companies that have leaders with both a vibrant, clear vision of where they are going and who have connected their employees to the bigger picture through their mission statement. The winners will be companies that have leaders in sync with their employees on a similar mission.

One of the most fun vacations any family can take is a trip to the happiest place on earth, Disney World. Walt Disney was the master of creating a vision for the future. From the very start, Walt developed a broad, overarching statement that has stood the test of time on a global basis: "To make people happy." This vision was then coupled with a mission statement that connects everyone with the "business plan":

"The Mission of the Walt Disney Company is to be one of the world's leading producers and providers of entertainment and information, using its portfolio of brands to differentiate our content, services, and consumer products." It was made clear by this statement that the Walt Disney Company mission was to develop the most creative, innovative, and profitable entertainment experiences and related products in the world.

But is this enough? No. The glue that binds the vision and mission together is a culture *based on values*. Returning to Disney, it is their values and ethics that make the "happiness sauce" come alive. Five essential components of the Disney culture are; innovation (remember, Mickey Mouse was the first cartoon presentation to have synchronized sound); maintaining a high standard of excellence in everything they do; commitment to positive inclusive ideas about family; they provide employment for all ages, timeless storytelling that delights and inspires and, finally, Disney is dedicated to honor, respect, and decency in order to inspire trust in the company.

This book's mission then is to provide you with vision and direction, to navigate and prosper in today's transparent world and, to help you develop your values based on a cultural foundation. This values-based journey begins by identifying and understanding the *Central Values System* of your company, employees, and business partners. Survey the landscape: What's the terrain? What's the climate? Conditions and forecasts? We will instill a sense of confidence behind the wheel, purposeful direction, as well as practical data tools that you'll discover are essential to meeting the objectives of all of those on board: customers, shareholders, employees, and suppliers.

The Central Values System is a navigation device—a vital component of business development and growth. This is not just getting the pulse. This system methodically and quantitatively identifies any disconnect between management, employees, suppliers, and customers. Beyond that, successful development and implementation of this system reflects a clear, unobstructed view to those "on the outside looking in," *potential* customers, employees, suppliers, and investors. The collective "you" will be sending a strong signal—a consistent message that resonates in a transparent world.

In chapter two we used the Welty Building Company and Akron Children's Hospital as an example of how emotionally intelligent leadership gets amazing results. The project came in at $178.5 million versus the projected $240 million. The code name for this project was "Building on the Promise," the project was designed to address the hospital's significant growth in patient volumes and services offered.

Before Welty was awarded the project, ACH asked one final question, "How do you create alignment with the entire building team and ensure they will build our vision as well as conduct themselves with our values during the construction process?" What was Welty's promise? The standard answer to these questions on a project that would have thousands of different workers is simple—"We put a schedule together, used technology, and held everyone accountable."

Welty takes a different approach—they talk about the fact that they have a totally transparent building process with open financial books. They take no profit and their building partners take no profit, unless the project comes in at financial target. They treat the team with respect dignity and a voice. They focus not just on the cost of construction but also on the ongoing cost of the building for the next fifty years and the costs of the building to the planet—the earth. They hire a building team that is like-minded in building a structure the right way—a building process that will produce the maximum result for the patients of ACH. Welty focuses on facilitating collaboration with the entire building team and making decisions during the construction process that respect the long-term health of the planet. Welty creates alignment by focusing on the triple bottom line—Profit, People, and Planet.

It's tough to maximize business potential if those involved with your success don't have the same values and vision. Conflicting opinions and perspectives can impede progress. *Creative* conflict, however, can be an opportunity to build consensus, develop new strategies, and benefit from negotiated compromise. We all appreciate it when we feel our voice has been heard. People and businesses thrive in a compatible world where the environment and people surrounding them are consistent and attuned. Businesses need internal consistency. So do the individuals within the organization as well as business partners and customers. Without that consistency there is discordance and dissonance.

The Cognitive Dissonance Theory was proposed by psychologist Leon Festinger. The theory was centered on how people attempt to reach internal consistency. Festinger suggested that people have an inner need to ensure that their beliefs and behaviors are congruent. People strive to avoid conflicting or inconsistent beliefs because they lead to disharmony. In Festinger's book, *A Theory of Cognitive Dissonance*, he said, "Cognitive dissonance can be seen as an antecedent condition which leads to activity oriented toward dissonance reduction just as hunger leads toward activity oriented toward hunger reduction."

The Central Values System gets to the core of discordance and dissonance in your business world to: 1) identify where there is congruence and where there are conflicting values, 2) measure and pinpoint where and to what degree incompatibilities exist and, 3) implement actionable steps to reduce discordance. This is an all-inclusive study of employees, suppliers, and customers.

So how do we get there from here? Well-planned surveys are essential. Now, wait. Before we go on, if your reaction to this is: "Oh surveys—been there, done that, useless, passé, boring," then you've already experienced the exact reason why these *are* important, and are a critical component of the Central Values System.

Surveys for a survey's sake are pointless time-wasters. Beyond that, survey results that aren't acted on and sharing results to some degree, and "in spirit" with participants is morale-lowering at best. You've probably participated in more than your fair share of these types of surveys. What was your reaction? Was it something such as, "Why do they bother asking? They will never do anything about it." So have your customers, suppliers, and employees. We are not going there. We're taking you down a different road—one that is much more strategic, measurable, and actionable. We will sharpen your focus of where relationships and understandings are incongruent, as well as how to realign them. You'll find that the intent, development, implementation, and interpretation of surveys within the Central Values System will identify issues obstructing business success. Even if your business is currently a well-oiled success machine, you'll uncover subtle and not-so-subtle impediments to even greater success.

Now let's get specific. These well-defined surveys are crucial measurement tools, and the Central Values System is the algorithm, unique to your organization and suppliers, that *motivates alignment of Terminal Values* and *Central Values*. Surveys are designed for you to implement; to establish the *average* baseline of the company's overall Terminal Values—your general business climate. These average baselines are markers that identify the degrees to which the values of your company's leadership, employees, customers, and partners align with the overall Terminal Values. These are specific to *your* industry, company, employees, and business partners and not a "one size fits all."

So to gauge your baseline, we'll demonstrate not just how to identify and treat symptoms but also how to take actionable steps that can lead to restoring the health and prosperity of your business. In the transparent world we use diagnostic testing to determine where the body is out of alignment. This baseline testing is referred to as "Centered Values"—the alignment of shared values, expectations, and aspirations of the employees, customers, and business partners.

Centered Values Diagnostic

Surveys begin with the company leadership team to establish a baseline, prior to being taken by employees, customers, and suppliers. The survey is broken into four categories: People, Community, Planet, and Communication. Each category incorporates a series of questions that are weighted on a scale from one to ten, with ten being the greatest value.

The values are rolled up into weighted averages, which are then compared to the overall company baseline of performance in each respective category. Each category will illustrate if and, if so, how far off center those surveyed are from the company baseline.

The aggregate roll-up provides a clear perspective of the overall health of the company. This assessment is essential to understand the relationships between the "critical mass"—company leadership, employees, suppliers, and business partners—

where there is congruence and where there is disharmony. This undistorted view provides a significant window of opportunity to assess, align, and reevaluate perspectives, opinions, and objectives on a global, transparent scale. What we found were the four pillars of a transparent company are: how they treat *people* and *communicate*, as well as interface with the *community* and *planet*.

Survey Questions

People *(Rate on a scale from 1–10)*

How important is it to the leadership of your company that employees, suppliers, customers have:

_____ Respect

_____ Dignity

_____ A Voice

Communication *(Rate on a scale from 1–10)*

How important is it to the leadership of your company that employees, suppliers, and customers have communication that is:

_____ Open

_____ Based on integrity

_____ Based on the company's vision and greater purpose

Community *(Rate on a scale from 1–10)*

How important is it to your company that employees, suppliers, customers have:

_____ A feeling of community with the company

_____ Do good in the community

_____ Are respected in the community

Planet *(Rate on a scale from 1–10)*

How important is it to your company that employees, suppliers, customers:

_____ Participate in programs to better the environment

_____ Recycle

_____ Have a plan to reduce their water usage and carbon footprint

_____ Survey Results

People

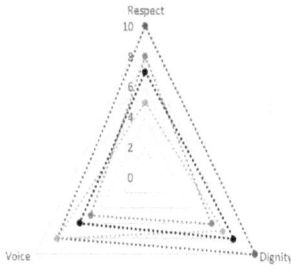

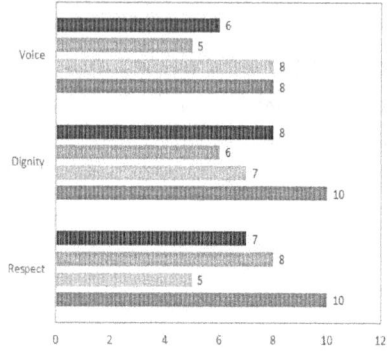

Communication

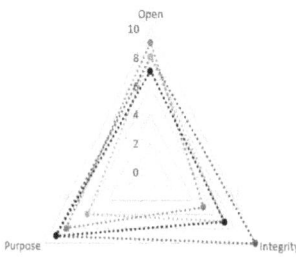

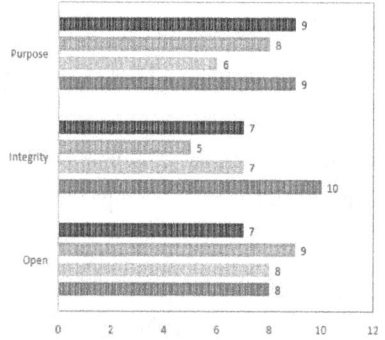

Community

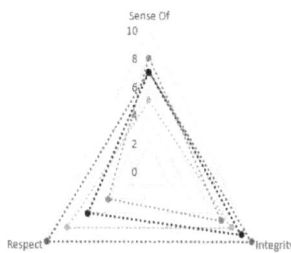

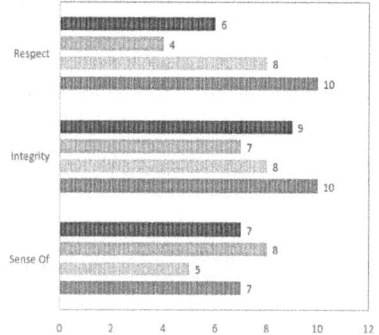

Planet

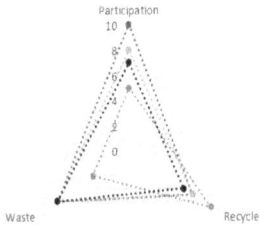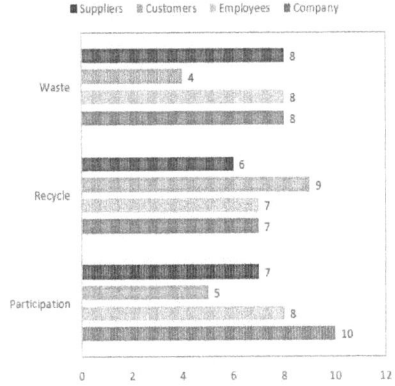

Survey Summary (Aggregate Roll-Up)

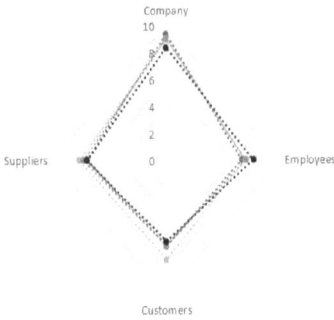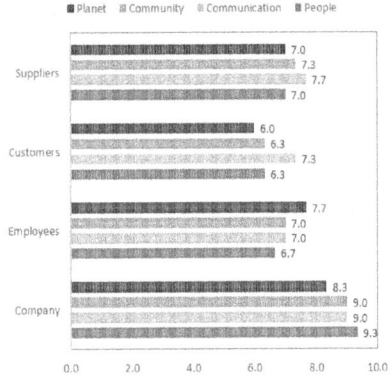

Getting Back to Center—Filling the Gap

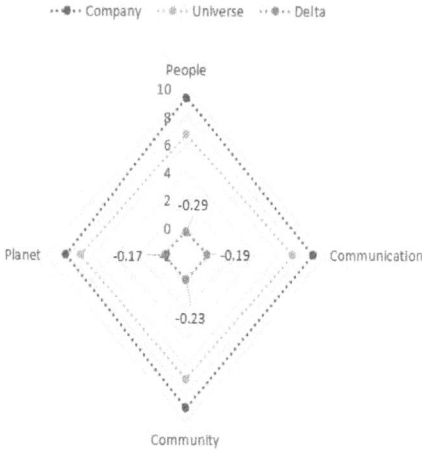

Depending on the degree off-center, Human Resources will prescribe a solution and work with the management team to determine the pathway for employees to "get back to center" in line with the company's Terminal Values. Related departments within the business will outline and develop strategies for alignment with customers and business partners.

This "balancing act" with the Centered Values Diagnostic for the basic alignment of shared values, expectations, and aspirations of the employees, customers, and business partners is important. It is also the starting point in developing a strong alignment of your company and in establishing a foundation for growth.

Chapter 4
Glass Company Compass
with Chuck Sarka

There is a frog and a scorpion on one side of the river. The frog's getting ready to cross the river and the scorpion says, "I'd really like to get over to the other side."

The frog looked at the scorpion and said, "Are you out of your mind?"

The scorpion says again, "Put me on your back and we'll swim across."

The Frog says again, "Scorpions sting. When scorpions sting, frogs die. Why would I put you on my back?"

The scorpion says, "That's kind of stupid that you asked me that, frog. If I sting you halfway across the river, we're both going to die because I can't swim."

The frog thinks about it for a minute, and then says, "Okay, yeah."

The frog puts the scorpion on his back and begins swimming across the river. They're talking to each other and, about halfway across the river, *whack!* The scorpion stings him.

The frog looks back and says, "What the hell? We're both going to die now. Why the hell did you do that?"

The scorpion says, "Because that's what I do. I'm a scorpion. I sting."

—Popular fable/allegory

So what criteria guides companies in the transparent world with whom you do business? As leaders, how do we know we are making the right decision that will help our teams flourish? Sixty-one percent of the business leaders in our survey attribute their success to making human connections ahead of setting goals and accomplishing tasks.

The way these business leaders connected was by sharing the leader's vision and values for the company. The leader's focus on helping to create a flourishing environment within the organization was a key for employee, customer, and supplier engagement. The bottom line with this statistic is that business owners, regardless of their aspirations, recognize the value of connecting with people—employees, shareholders, suppliers, or customers.

In the transparent world we give up control of our company's message. Individuals take the message, they share it and it grows. If we pick the right employees, customers, and suppliers, they will share our vision and values with the world and our company will flourish.

To assist you in picking the right partners and navigating your journey in the transparent world we are going to introduce two simple tools to help: the Glass Values Decision Diagnostic and the Pinch Model.

Glass Values Decision Diagnostic

Over the years we cannot begin to count the endless hours spent sitting in meetings discussing and contemplating issues such as an employee's future, whether we should continue to do business with XYZ Company, or if we should buy or merge with ABC group; "Will it be a successful marriage?" All of these discussions had two simple fundamentals in common, though, at the time we failed to recognize them for what they were. Instead, we tried to analyze and justify our decisions based on SWOT analyses, how the balance sheet looked, where a plot landed in a nine-blocker matrix according to some formula, or some other empirical scrutiny. The two simple fundamentals we were missing at the time were the Value Add and Centered Values. When combined with the well-known analyses we all use every day, they not only make many decisions more likely to be successful, they make decisions transparent and less time consuming.

The traditional way of looking at the decision to hire or fire is based on a desire to perform and employee job knowledge.

A very close mentor and friend of mine, Dan Lumpkin (www.lumpkinassociates.com) uses the weed the garden model to vet what course of action should be taken to help with employee performance. The x-axis was desire to perform and the y-axis was job knowledge. When you find yourself with an employee who displays both a low desire to perform coupled with low job knowledge; it's time to weed the garden!

In today's global fast-paced world, the gardens we play in now consist of multiple, vast acres, infested with various forms of "weeds." To deal with this we need a high powered "weed whacker" that not only deals with employees but customers, vendors, and situations; where we are trying to evaluate whether the relationship we are about to enter into is right or wrong. We propose that the Glass Values Decision Matrix is the tool that just might prevent your garden from getting weeds.

The Glass Values Decision Matrix uses the two principles of Value Added along with Centered Values to shape a simple matrix:

Value Added is the unassuming concept of asking whether the party you are partnering with will add value, is adding, or is likely to continue to add value to the relationship. In the transparent world you add more value when you actively co-create to make things better for People, Planet, and Profit—the triple bottom line. It is your farm and tractor, so the ultimate definition of value added is up to you and your company.

Centered value is the alignment of shared values, expectations, and aspirations of the employees, customers, and business partners. The categories that the Glass Company aligns around are People, Planet, Communication, and Community. It all comes down to this: do your employees, customers, and suppliers believe what you believe? Do they value what you value?

The Glass VALUES Decision Matrix
Employees, Suppliers, and Customers

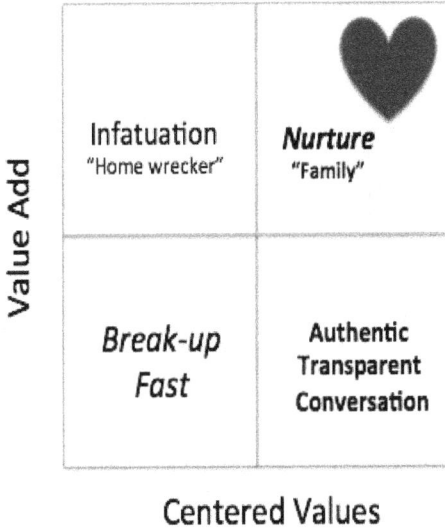

Infatuation "Home wrecker"	Nurture "Family"
Break-up Fast	Authentic Transparent Conversation

Value Add (vertical axis)

Centered Values (horizontal axis)

Using the matrix with these concepts in mind, a situation where there is both high value-add and high correlation of centered values; love abounds and everything should be done to nurture and continue the relationship. This is the "band of brothers" category, Family. If you find yourself contemplating or in a relationship where centered values are there but the value add is missing; an authentic transparent conversation is needed to reset expectations. On the other end of the spectrum, where the value add is there, the centered values are missing. We contend that you are more than likely infatuated with the situation—with long-term sustainability of the relationship minimal at the best, destructive at the worst. Finally, like in the weed the garden model, low value, added and low centered values break up fast. Run from this situation. It can only lead to both a cultural and financial nightmare!

Next time you find yourself agonizing over a decision, stop and ask yourself if this situation is going to add value to your journey and if the centered values have been established to ensure a sustainable relationship. These partners are going to be telling my story.

The Pinch in a Transparent World

The *Pinch Model* was originally developed by Sherwood & Glidewell to provide a strategy for *staying out* of trouble rather than *getting out* of trouble with your employees. The Pinch Model says that every relationship either at home, work, or play sooner or later will result in a "Pinch." In a transparent world we needed to have a Pinch Model in place for our customers, employees, and suppliers to lead.

The truth is a better solution—even if it is negative. Studies show that a key driver of brand loyalty is when a customer's expectation is not initially met and the company does what it takes to meet the customer's expectation. The key to any relationship is to address these pinches immediately, and have a process in place to handle issues before they get to a relationship-destroying crunch. In the transparent world, if we do not deal with the pinch before it becomes a crunch it is posted to the Internet as a negative comment, which is viewed forever.

Rosanna Shah, a stay-at-home mother in Denham Springs, Louisiana, says her daughter developed a "very red, very hot" rash after using one of the new diapers she bought. Ms. Shah posted her complaints on the Pampers Web site and called the company. Unhappy with the response, Ms. Shah started a Facebook crusade. Her page, titled "Pampers, Bring Back the Old Cruisers/Swaddlers," quickly reached seven thousand members, doubled its membership in a week's time, and continued to gain support. "P&G is trying to insinuate that all babies get diaper rashes and that we're making a mountain out of a molehill," says Ms. Shah. "That's when people got mad" (Byron, 2010).

Today, a single online post on a merchandise or consumer website can influence millions of customers' purchases. A Nielson global advertising survey reported that 92 percent of consumers around the world say that recommendations from friends and family, more than any other form of advertising, influence purchases, while 70 percent trust online consumer reviews. Newspapers, magazines, and television scored below 50 percent (Nielson, 2011).

Gathering Data and Sharing, Clarifying Expectations: At the beginning of a relationship we discuss what we expect in the relationship and define the parameters of our expectations for both parties. It's the honeymoon period, a time where both parties are open to exciting new possibilities. We need to review with each new employee, supplier, or customer what we expect him or her to bring to our organization, and what he or she can expect from our organization. As a leader you should also ask, "How can I help you be better?" and "What do you need from me?"

Role Clarity and Commitment: The next step in your relationship is the everyday interface where you clarify roles and commitments. Both parties are meeting expectations. You are doing what you said you would do and I am doing what I said I would do in the relationship. We are both growing the relationship based on shared moments of positive connection.

Trust: This is where we enjoy a period in our relationship where we can count on each other, where our word is our bond, and where we can reasonably predict each other's behavior in most situations. This is an opportunity to broaden and build relationships based on centered values.

The Pinch, Choice Point: A *"Pinch"* is a moment of emotional discomfort. Imagine a time when an article of clothing was twisted, or you put your watch on the wrong wrist. While the feeling you have physically is not painful, it is definitely *not comfortable.* This is the same thing that happens emotionally when we experience a pinch in our relationship. A pinch happens when the other person's behavior becomes different than our original expectation. The expected behavior, or what we think should be the expected behavior, does not happen. A pinch can also be when the other person's behavior is totally out of character. We notice it and many times do not speak about it or address it, hoping it will go away or change back to the way it was—the way we "expect it to be." We also may rationalize that maybe we do not perceive what is going on instead. We might even avoid the issue, feeling it is the best thing. Perceive

Planned Reconciliation: This works best from the moment we first perceive a pinch to exist in our relationship. We can avoid many of the crunches in relationships of our life *if we will learn to speak up at the pinch.* A post or an online chat from your company enables this in the transparent world. At this moment we are less defensive, more understanding, and more accepting of each other's concerns about our relationship than we will likely be after ambiguity and uneasiness begins. Be authentic, truthful, and be real. Always speak up at the pinches, renegotiate expectations, say what you want to have happen in your relationship and reach a new agreement on the mutual interests involved. Tell those you work with and those you love that "if you have a pinch with me, *I will stop whatever I am doing* or where I am going and we will interact and talk, text, or post about the pinch." The speed and reach at which information travels in the transparent world can damage a company or person in an instant. You and your company need a process and technology in place to put the relationship back on track. Let them know you will listen and spend whatever time is needed to keep the pinch from becoming a crunch. It is that important. Dealing with an issue at the time of the pinch saves a lifetime of negative posts.

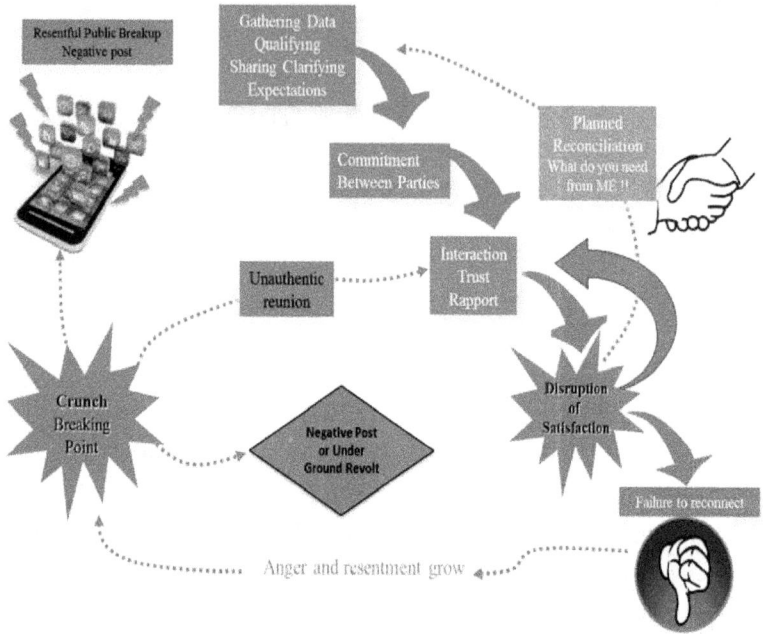

THE Glass Company *PINCH* MODEL

Resentful Public Breakup
Negative post

Gathering Data
Qualifying
Sharing Clarifying
Expectations

Commitment
Between Parties

Planned
Reconciliation
What do you need
from ME !!

Unauthentic
reunion

Interaction
Trust
Rapport

Crunch
Breaking
Point

Negative Post
or Under
Ground Revolt

Disruption
of
Satisfaction

Failure to reconnect

Anger and resentment grow

Chapter 5
Team Intelligence—TQ
Making Teams Work in a Transparent World
with Solange Charas

A kindly, old stranger was walking through the land when he came upon a village. As he entered, the villagers moved toward their homes locking doors and windows. The stranger smiled and asked why all the villagers are so frightened.

"I am a simple traveler, looking for a soft place to stay for the night and a warm place for a meal."

There's not a bite to eat in the whole province, he was told. "We are weak and our children are starving. Better keep moving on."

The stranger said that he had everything he needed, and he was just thinking of making some stone soup to share with all of them. He pulled an iron cauldron from his cloak, filled it with water, and began to build a fire under it. *Next, with* great ceremony, he drew an ordinary-looking stone from a silken bag and dropped it into the water. By now, hearing the rumor of food, most of the villagers had come out of their homes or watched from their windows. As the stranger sniffed the "broth" and licked his lips in anticipation, hunger began to overcome their fear.

"Ahh," the stranger said to himself rather loudly, "I do like a tasty stone soup. Of course, stone soup with cabbage, that's hard to beat."

Soon a villager approached hesitantly, holding a small cabbage he'd retrieved from its hiding place, and added it to the pot. "Wonderful!!" cried the stranger. "You know, I once had stone soup with cabbage and a bit of salt beef as well, and it was fit for a king."

The village butcher managed to find some salt beef. And so it went, potatoes, onions, carrots, mushrooms were added to the cauldron until there was indeed—a delicious meal for everyone in the village to share. The villager elder offered the stranger a great deal of money for the "magic" stone, but he refused to sell it. On his way out of the village, the stranger came upon a group of village children standing near the road. He gave the silken bag containing the stone to the youngest child and whispered "It was not the stone, but the villagers that had performed the magic."

The moral of the story: By working together for the benefit of all involved, a greater outcome is achieved than people working alone.

> The whole is greater than the sum of the parts.
>
> —Aristotle, 350 BCE

Another way to look at transparency in your organization is from a team perspective. This chapter will describe the "new science of teams"—transforming our ability to understand and manage teams from the subjective to the objective, based on evidence and proven interventions. We'll address why great teams are so critical to business success in the transparent world. We will share findings that clearly demonstrate that companies that have a culture of "getting along" teams versus "getting ahead" teams show greater financial results and employee engagement.

We'll also explain the economic underpinnings of why transparency in teams is so critical and, lastly, we'll provide a description of the team intelligence (TQ) assessment where you'll get a chance take a short assessment of the quality of your team. Team effectiveness in the transparent world is the new business imperative—it's the way most organizations hope to generate success. But how can we consistently create and manage high-performing teams across every area and level in the organization?

Why should we even care about how well teams perform? It's simple—teams are part of our everyday lives at work (and home, for that matter). With more than 82 percent of US companies reporting that they rely on teams to get things done (and that number is growing annually), it's likely that you work for one of the 10.6 million businesses that rely on teams to generate results [Ref. 34]. More than 62 percent of knowledge-workers report that they are on at least one team at work, and some researchers estimate that up to 95 percent of employees are on at least one team [Ref. 35]. This translates into more than 87 million people who have to work with others to get things done [Ref. 36]. If you're not already on at least one team at work, you will be soon, and will probably be asked to serve on more than one team in the future. Teams are here to stay and will be a prominent part of your workday.

Team as an Emotional Experience

Let's do a little experiment. Think about a time when you were on a successful team. What's the first thing you remember? Make a mental list of some words that describe your experience. Most likely, you thought about how you felt — the positive experience you had when you were on this "great team."

When describing experiences on a great team, the majority of people I interviewed faces lit up when describing a general sense of well being, passion, optimism, camaraderie, and high energy. What's interesting is they describe the team's successes as a mere afterthought, as if it were implicit that great teams would have a long list of accomplishments. Here's a bonus: people who experience being on a great team tend to stay in contact with their team members long after the team is disbanded, saying that they want to extend the feelings of success and connectedness as long as possible.

If success in business is a function of the relationships you make, nothing can be more powerful in sustaining relationships than having a great team experience.

Now think of a time when you were on a dysfunctional team. What experiences are you remembering now and what are the words that describe your experience? Most people report feelings of frustration, disappointment, impatience, and powerlessness. They sometimes were even angry at wasting precious time with people who couldn't effectively work together to get things done. Even if the team accomplished something, their poor experience took away from the sense of accomplishment, even if the team achieved their goals. What's alarming is that most people report having been on many more dysfunctional teams than high-performing teams in their careers.

Why is the team experience so powerful in evoking both positive and negative feelings? Why are high-performing teams so rare? What is that special "magic" that transforms a collection of people into a high-performing, dynamic, exciting, and successful team? Intuitively and experientially we know high-performing teams deliver high-quality results, and research shows the relationship between high-performing teams and an organization's success.

In my own experience, as a twenty-five-year veteran of the HR function, as a consultant, C-Suite executive, and board director, I have, for the most part, been on and seen dysfunctional teams. Most leaders/managers know the incredible power of a team, but are at a loss for how to create and manage every team so that it can be high-performing.

Frustrated about the lack of technology or science in creating and managing teams to high performance, I focused on this topic in my PhD research. Creating a way to understand the "white space" between people that was believed to generate great team experiences and transform low-performing teams into high-performing teams was the goal. What accounted for high-performing teams and, more importantly, what were the economic consequences of team performance? Measuring the ROI of teams, I learned, would be an important value proposition. Fundamentally, these questions were explored and answered: What makes great teams great? Could we create a "blueprint" for generating high-performing teams? What financial impact does this have on a company's bottom line?

The Focus Should be on Getting Along, *Not* Getting Ahead

Traditionally, our focus on getting ahead has been on individual success, we don't understand how we impact the system. Changing this focus is critical. A recent study found that organizations who value, recognize, and encourage a culture that promotes getting along versus a strong culture of getting ahead are performing better. They value honesty, trust, morality, altruism, team-mindedness, a focus on others, personal benefit and, in the end, they not only get things done, they do so with engaged employees. The old school style of management—more consistent with the getting ahead approach—rewards power and control, manipulation of others, self-interest, unbridled assertiveness, lack of empathy, self-promotion, and the culture of winning at all costs. These values generate competition in the workplace and foster an environment of distrust. Typically, people keep information to themselves, as information is the basis of power and the anathema to transparency.

Here's the powerful finding—you might think the "getting ahead" style would drive economic success since the organization is focused on winning at all costs. However, this set of studies shows that getting along cultures are associated with 10.6 percent higher ROI and 5.7 percent higher ROA than organizations with "getting ahead" cultures [Ref. 37].

Transparent organizations seem to perform better financially than those that are not open and forthcoming in their endeavors. And there's more: the "getting along" organizations reflect the value system of the Millennials. Why is this important? Because by the year 2025, Millennials will make up the majority of the workforce. We need to find a way to engage with and communicate to their value-system. The predominant themes that describe Millennials include: they celebrate diversity, they are entrepreneurial and team players, they promote positive change, they are social, they have a commitment to society and, most important, experience and job satisfaction trump pay. If these attributes sound consistent with the getting along cultural themes, you're right, and that's why creating getting along organizational values and culture is so critical in attracting and engaging the Millennial workforce. The more we are able to create these values in our companies now, the more likely we are to recruit and retain this growing segment of the workforce, especially as we face a looming skilled labor shortage [Ref. 38]. Organizations that can attract Millennials will have the competitive advantage over organizations that can't.

Attributes of Team Dynamic, Team Effectiveness, Agreeableness, and CQ			
Team Dynamic	Team Effectiveness	CQ	Agreeableness
Engagement	Synergy	Meta-cognitive	Trust
Active Listening	Skills	Cognitive	Morality
Individuality	Quality	Motivation	Modesty
Relationality	Innovation	Behavioral	Altruism
Solidarity	Team Self-Belief		Team Mindedness
Understanding			Personal Benefit Focus
Action			
Planning			
Power & Influence			
Openness			

Other Factors that Impact Team Performance

It's no surprise that research on teams continues to produce interesting findings. Diversity, both in terms of race and gender, are strong drivers of team performance. One study showed that having racially diverse leadership is associated with better outcomes. This is due to the fact that diversity candidates have a heightened sensitivity to integrating the needs of multiple constituents [Ref. 39]. And when women are put on teams, the overall team performance improves, associated with a higher level of team collective intelligence [Ref. 40]. What we found was participants, both male and female, reported that teams with women on them tended to be more satisfying as an experience because women tend to be better listeners, are better able to draw others into conversations, and are less likely to dominate groups with their opinions, as proven through social sensitivity research [Ref. 41].

The Theory Underlying Team Transparency

Espousing that team transparency is "motherhood and apple pie" is fine; however, it is important to understand how high-TQ and transparent teams generate positive economic outcomes, and can be explained by two theories. The first is called Information Asymmetry Theory (IAT), developed by George Stigler [Ref. 42] and brought to the public eye by Nobel prize-winning Professor Joseph Stiglitz [Ref. 43-44]. IAT states that when one party has more or better information than the other, and is unwilling or unable to share this information, an imbalance of power occurs and this has a measurable economic opportunity cost. Information asymmetry is the opposite of "perfect information"—a key assumption in neo-classical economics. Where perfect information generates economic value, information asymmetry generates economic losses.

By minimizing information asymmetry in teams (measured by the TQ assessment), the team is able to generate a more robust exchange of ideas, better decision making, ability to achieve goals and, ultimately, higher levels of production and resulting profitability. When the climate in the team is not conducive to information sharing (low TQ levels), we observed poor financial performance in our executive research participants.

The second theory is based on knowledge creation, which is seen as *the* competitive advantage in our information-based economy. In his book, *The Knowledge-Creating Company*, [Ref. 46-47] Nonaka states that one of the fundamental reasons for business success isn't necessarily better costs of capital, manufacturing approaches, supplier relationships, or human capital management processes. Although all these are important, what is essential to business success is the ability of organizations to create new knowledge or the ability of a "company as a whole to create new knowledge, disseminate it throughout the organization, and embody it in product, services, and systems." Nonaka describes the knowledge-creation process resulting from team SECI or "Socialization, Externalization of ideas, Combination and Internalization of new knowledge." He claims that this process can only happen when a particular climate is present in the team, which he calls "ba" or the context that harbors meaning. Thus, ba is the shared space that serves as a foundation for knowledge creation, and is reflected in the TQ score.

The Fundamentals of Team—According to Charas

The two categories of team success—team dynamic quality and team effectiveness—together are a measure of the degree to which team members are able to reduce information asymmetry and is a measure of Ba—the container for knowledge creation. The research connects the dots between TQ in the executive management team and corporate financial performance, demonstrating that executive management teams are responsible for up to 20 percent of a firm's profitability. If you wanted to make a difference in the overall performance of the organization, start at the top. (See exhibit below.)

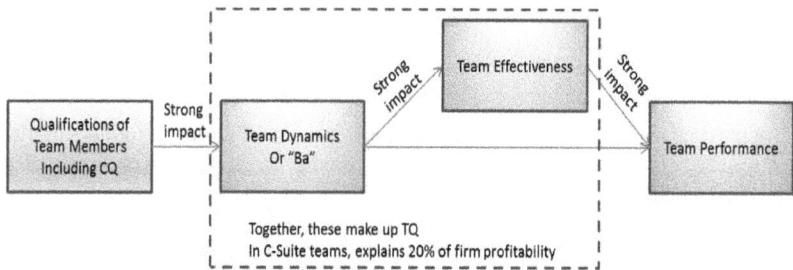

At the end of this chapter, you can take a TQ "mini-assessment" that will give you an indication of how your team performs against a few of these attributes. The sidebar lists the names and definitions of the TQ, Agreeableness, and Cultural Intelligence (CQ) attributes.

CQ is a measure of an individual's ability to understand and adapt appropriately to different cultures and it is a measure of a person's predisposition to working well in a team setting. The measure was originally developed by P. Christopher Early in the early 2000's to help organizations understand if an employee will be successful on an expatriate assignment. Today it is used more broadly, as Early stated that each organization has its own unique culture, and the instrument measures individual adaptability to cultural norms [Ref. 47]. To learn more about CQ and take a self-assessment, follow this link:

You can determine your own CQ—don't worry, CQ can be learned—so if you have low CQ scores, you can work on improving your ability to work effectively in teams and organizations.

Although not part of the TQ measure, in our client work we gather information on one additional indicator—Team Agreeableness. This measure allows us to understand the team's level of transparency. Agreeableness is a measure that was developed as part of the Big Five Personality Factor assessment, and captures the psychological profile of the team against the attributes listed in the sidebar on the previous page.

The unique value proposition of the dynamic quality aspect of the assessment tool is that it is "self-reflective"—members of the team express what they need to be high-performing. This means that an outsider isn't telling the team what they need and how they should perform. Instead, the team, as a collective, expresses through the assessment what is required for them to be high-performing. Each team creates its own blueprint for success, and that's why it is so compelling and effective as a tool.

What Now?

There are several ways you and your organization can benefit from using the TQ assessment to achieve greater transparency, higher-performing teams and, ultimately, higher-performing organizations.

Hiring new employees — The instrument can be used to profile the collective team aspirations of the organization and ensure that the people you're hiring share your values and aspirations when it comes to working with others;

Assigning current employees to existing teams — The instrument can be used when recruiting existing employees to a new or existing team and to understand if they are a good behavioral fit to that specific team.

Evaluating existing teams — The instrument can be used on existing teams in the organization to determine their TQ and identify appropriate interventions to improve TQ quality.

Engineering new teams in the organization (ad hoc, innovation, product, and so on) — The instrument can be used to create new and highly effective teams by matching the aspirations of team dynamic quality for all team members and eliminating the differences and productivity losses that arise from different people having different needs for the team to be successful. This is particularly important for ad hoc teams, product development teams, or innovation teams.

The Mini-Assessment

The following exercise makes up the mini-assessment. There are five statements to give you a sense of the team dynamics attribute and five statements focused on team effectiveness. You may also take this diagnostic at glasscompany.com.

Instructions

For team dynamic: Provide *two* answers per item for these five statements, once for actual experience and the second for desired experience. Actual experience is the way it is today. Desired experience is how you would like it to be if you were a high-performing team.

For team effectiveness: Provide one answer per item by indicating the extent to which you agree or disagree with the following statements as it describes your team.

1=Strongly disagree, 2=Disagree, 3=Neutral, 4=Agree, 5=Strongly Agree

---

Team Dynamic—Answer from 1 to 5, twice—Actual and Desired

_____/_____ Team members consider all sides of an issue before acting on it.

_____/_____ The team looks for guidance from one team member.

_____/_____ Team members take their time to listen before talking.

_____/_____ Team members are receptive and open-minded.

_____/_____ One team member makes the final decision for the team.

Team Effectiveness—Answer from 1 to 5

_____/_____ There is effective communication among team members.

_____/_____ Individuals are valued as team members.

_____/_____ There are measurable quality standards for outcomes in place that are regularly monitored.

_____/_____ All team members perform to the best of their ability.

_____/_____ Team member training and development needs are systematically identified.

Self-scoring Team Dynamic: If the difference between the "Actual" and "Desired" score is greater than 10 percent, you likely have a low TQ team. Team Effectiveness: If the average score for all five statements is less than 4.4, then your team performs below the average for the ninetieth percentile of performing teams.

Endnotes for survey

Lingham, Tony. Conversations as Core to Team Experiences: A JIT measurement and mapping system to facilitate team directed learning and development. ESADE, 2005.

Bateman, B., Wilson, F. C., and Bingham, D. (2002). "Team Effectiveness – Development of an Audit Questionnaire." *The Journal of Management Development,* 21(3), 215-226. doi: 10.1108/02621710210420282

Chapter 6
Love: The Other Four-Letter Word
That Drives Your Business
with Dr. William Paolillo

In 2013, Bizarre Voice, an aggregator of customer reviews for major retailers and industry, analyzed over a billion online posts. Of the 70 percent of these posts found to be neutral or positive, nearly 30 percent contained the word "love."

When I asked a CMO concerning how she felt about the online interaction she said, "Being a control freak it makes me nauseous . . . we understand to win we need to be on the Internet talking to our customers . . . we go with it, give up control." That is how you win in the transparent world.

The question is not if your customers, suppliers, and employees want to say they love your products, services, and even you on the Internet—it is how you make sure you have more lovers than haters.

How does business harness this disruptive power of the masses in a transparent world? How does business connect with customers, suppliers, and employees in an environment that's not motivated by the values we are taught in business school that should motivate them? How do leaders lead and people flourish in the new transparent world?

A number of years ago I was working and living in Ohio as a Senior Vice President of a $700-million-dollar business unit in an international, multibillion-dollar company. I was there to fix it and I was all about the numbers. I had a good team. We were all highly trained MBAs and six-sigma black belts. We tightened control and cut as well as shifted resources. And we measured everything—you get what you inspect. In two years, we restored our business unit to profitability for the first time in eight years. I was rightfully proud and on top of the corporate ladder. I was playing the game with rules I'd been taught and I was good at it. I was destined for bigger things.

The company as a whole missed a forecast and the CEO was sacked. My mother, who had been diagnosed with cancer the year before, came to me and said, "Billy I want you to come home, back to Long Island. I want to spend my last days with my son near me." My emotions were all over the place.

I decided to go back to Long Island and within two years sales in my former business unit were down more than 28 percent to below $500 million. What happened? I'd done everything right. All the things I was taught to do in business school did not produce sustainable results. My family, my personal life, and my worldview of business had been shaken. So what was I to do when I don't understand something and everything I thought I knew might be wrong? I studied it and devoted the pursuit of my doctorate at Case Western Reserve University to find some answers.

I started my doctoral studies focused on how to maximize sales and profit by understanding the pricing mechanism of a company. What I found was the four-letter word that drives sustainable success in a company in the transparent world is not cash, but another four-letter word—*love*. What I found is that business success is all about being transparent, connected, and understanding that we have little to no control. The way business achieves sustainable double-digit growth rates in sales and profit, is to co-create with your customers, employees, and suppliers. If you set your customers, employees, and suppliers free to tell your story, they will grow your sales and profit.

It's passé to say that the Internet has disrupted business. Less understood is how different organizations are using different approaches with varying degrees of success and what disruptions these uses are causing in how business is conducted on the Internet.

Profit may drive business, but as study after study shows that profit is not a primary motivator for people that and the Internet has given voice to the individual.

Wikipedia is a perfect example. It's an encyclopedia considered the most comprehensive repository of knowledge in the world that is produced exclusively by people providing content and editing for free. It has flourished where the traditionally-based and massively-funded Microsoft Encarta version of the encyclopedia has failed. In an information economy, where an individual can broadcast knowledge, opinion, or innovative ideas, the idea of "disruption," is the key to business success.

In this research, we've traversed all types of companies and interviewed individuals in organizations from $150 million to $5 billion and from the CEO to the customer service agent to the construction worker on jobsites. We followed up our interviews with a massive online survey to validate what we found in our interviews. Looking for motivators other than money and profit, we asked: What do organizations do that get people to say positive things about them and their people during an online interaction? By better understanding the customer interaction, we found that a company's default reaction was much like mine as a Senior Vice President: the typical company response attempts to take control of the online interaction in an effort to end the conversation and avoid negative feedback.

More successful organizations, however, do something very different. They give up a great deal of control and jointly create something new—they co-create online with their customers and employees. What's interesting is that these organizations recognize that their online customers are not the final recipients of their message. Online, customers are a bridge for their message—a means for broad dissemination enabled by the Internet. Even more interesting—what I call customer love—is how these companies are rewarded. They are described as "love" in the customers' own words, as

47

shown by their affective expressions online. Seventy percent of the posts online about a product or service are found to be neutral or positive and nearly 30 percent contained the word "love." What does that word mean to you? When do you use it? Does it inspire you to action? Customer love is a huge opportunity for organizations.

We found that when organizations interact online and co-create with individuals, the factors that most resonate create a sense of trust, self-efficacy, empathy, and authenticity, as well as shared control. The organizations were rewarded with "Online Customer Love."

For love to exist, an individual must first feel a sense of security and trust. Trust is when one makes oneself vulnerable to receiving information. The emotional "contagion" created by the online interaction in an organization's everyday customer interactions is an opportunity to build and broaden the relationship. These factors engender "online customer love" and build an organization's brand and business.

What is online customer love? It's a positive expression from an individual when he or she is at the keyboard and the person has had an experience with you, your company, or an individual talking about your product or service. Now, why does it matter? In the past, if people wanted to complain or wanted to compliment, what would they do? They would send a letter. Remember those letters that came in? If it was a bad letter, you'd deal with it one on one. Now, when the complaint is made, it's posted online. You don't control where it is posted, or when. That customer interaction is what your products and services become. We are what our customers say about us. Your customer's perception is your reality.

We found that company leaders who understood that it was about their customers, their employees, and suppliers maximized their online customer love. The company set them free and let the individual be in control during the online interaction. The company is no longer in control—the voice provided by the Internet has put the customer in control.

We interviewed leaders in a number of companies. One of the best stories was Goo Gone. Their product removes sticky, gooey mess from just about everything—from Harley Davidson motorcycles to grills. They took their product and sent it out to their customers—bloggers. They said, "Okay, let's see what happens."

What happened was amazing. The best story is the Harley story. They sent it to a blogger of Harley Davidson Motorcycles and gave him a Harley jacket. The makers of Goo Gone used magic marker on the back of this jacket. (The product can remove magic marker.)

The first thing the blogger did was to create a video. He said, "You can't believe what these guys from Goo Gone did. First of all, they sent me this jacket." The video showed his removing the magic marker. Then he went on to show how it removes tar from the fenders on a Harley." What did the makers of Goo Gone do? They trusted. By trusting, they were rewarded with online customer love.

In our online survey we not only validated our first findings but found two distinct mechanisms that work together to create a positive post online from individuals for a company. The two mechanisms are online co-creation and a company being playful during the online interaction.

Online co-creation (OCC) is the interaction between an individual and an organization that creates value for both parties, as evidenced by at least one reposting of an online exchange. There are four distinct parts of online co-creation: OCC Advocacy, OCC Help, OCC Personal Interaction, and OCC Seek/Share.

We [Ref. 48] define a company being playful as being open, flexible, creative, spontaneous, and playful during the online interaction. We tested the survey data using Structured Equation Modeling to determine how companies create a positive online post.

We found Online Co-Creation and Play explained 52 percent of why an individual posted a positive comment online. The combination of studies told us that to create more positive online posts—"online customer love"—a company leaders must create an environment where customers, employees, and influencers can co-create in a playful environment. The use of behaviors such as authenticity, empathy, and building self-efficacy provide further fuel to create a connection with the customer.

In our quantitative study, Online Co-Creation explained 35 percent of online customer love. Our explanation of online customer love increased to 53 percent from our sample, when we added a company being open, flexible, imaginative, spontaneous, creative, and playful during their online interaction. Being playful describes our concept of "control with." From our qualitative research we found that an organization's default reaction was to attempt to "control over" (www.sciencedirect.com/science/article/pii/0361368279900175, accessed May 26, 2015) the online interaction in an effort to end the conversation and avoid negative feedback. More successful organizations will do something very different. They give up a great deal of control and jointly create something new—they co-create online with their customers and employees.

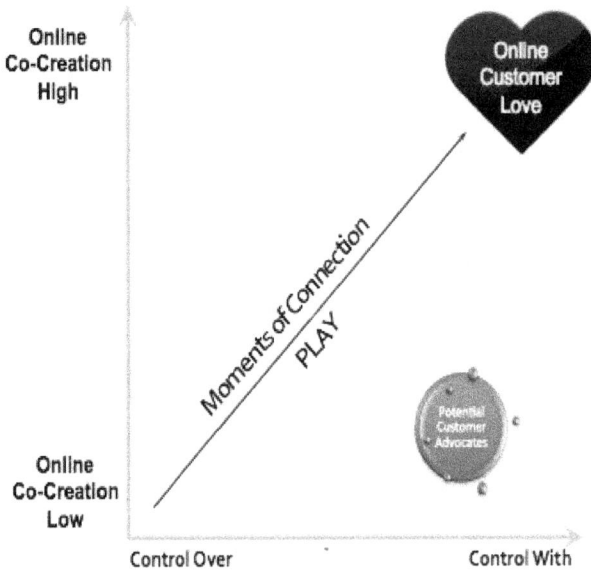

The interaction of online co-creation and control as depicted illustrates how a company increases the online expressed customer love. The company, relevant partners, and the customer allow for a strategic orientation that informs the tactical "Four P's to activate the company's customer advocates." *Products* are viewed in terms of service flows in which the service is provided directly or indirectly through an object. *Promotion* is reoriented toward conversation and dialog with the customer. *Price* is replaced with a value proposition created by both sides of the exchange. *Place* is supplanted with value networks and processes
(www.link.springer.com/article/10.1007/s11747-007-0069-6 accessed 5/23/2015)

When organizations choose to co-create their online content with customers, they amplify online co-creation and increase positive customer affect. Organizations focus on collaborating with customers to produce and sustain value.

We also discovered that what we think works to create customer goodwill and a friendly environment in the *physical* world does not necessarily work *online*.

During a face-to-face customer interaction friendly service is a positive differentiator. Just think about your morning stop at your local Starbucks. First, you think of it as "your" Starbuck's; they engage in a short, friendly conversation. For example: "How are you, Bill? Having the usual?" They smile and they are just nice. This shared moment of positivity is what creates positive affect in face-to-face interactions and we are likely to share that experience with our friends by word-of-mouth. The same should hold true for online conversations, right? Wrong.

We found that when organizations conduct their online interaction in a polite, structured fashion, the effect is a reduction in the "online love" the customer shows the organization. When a company is trying to be polite, courteous, kind, and friendly it is perceived as inauthentic due to the flat medium of text during the online interaction. Authenticity, keeping it real, is a key factor in helping to create online customer love.

The Internet has created a transparent world that has disrupted business. Now the way business is being conducted on the Internet is being disrupted. Organizations that recognize customers as a bridge to broadcast and enhance their message, and not simply as recipients of a pre-packaged message, are rewarded online with customer love. Love is no longer a four-letter word in business; it is the disruption that will create sustainable business growth with our customers, suppliers, and employees.

Chapter 7
How to Get Your Story Told
in a Transparent World
with Dr. David Grogan

I realized the importance of having a story today is what really separates companies. People don't just wear our shoes, they tell our story.
—Blake Mycoskie CEO, Tom's Shoes [Ref. 49]

Storytelling is the game. It's what we all do. It's why Nike is Nike, it's why Apple is Apple, it's why Walt Disney built Disney World, and it's why Vince McMahon makes a billion dollars.
—Gary Vaynerchuk Entrepreneur, Author [Ref. 50]

There are a few things we want you to take away from this piece. Your story is no longer just your story. Suppliers, customers, and employees create and distribute it for you. Companies who do well build stories that involve and inspire their constituents. Your company's growth will come from referrals by your customers, employees, and suppliers. Good companies recognize their customers as a conduit for enabling and spreading their message—a means for broad dissemination enabled by the Internet and other media in our information rich on demand society. Recognizing how your customers think and creating personal and platform-specific messages will lead to interactions that not only facilitate the distribution of your story, but also lead to better, co-created stories. If you build your brand through and around compelling stories, you will build a very powerful brand.

The idea that storytelling is central to human understanding is as old as history itself. Stories shape the sense of who we are, from where our ancestors lived to what the future holds. Our identities, habits, and aspirations form largely through the chronicles and accounts we find compelling. If you discount the importance of storytelling, given the dynamic times we're living in, and if the mention of storytelling puts the image of campfires, clubs, and Cro-Magnon man into your head, you're not alone. Nevertheless, you must reconsider. The notion that storytelling is no longer relevant could not be farther from the truth. In today's on-line, attention-deficit world, the stories that represent you and your company are more important than ever. They must be precise, persuasive, and promising if they are to be profitable. The difference is that you are telling your story so someone else can spread it on the Internet. Our objective is to provide perspective on the importance of the stories you're telling and to suggest ways to think about the various stakeholders who will hear, digest, and spread your message. This is the key to winning in the new transparent world.

To be effective, your stories must have quality content in context that disparate target populations can appreciate. They must address the intellectual and emotional needs of your audience and inspire them to believe in and be part of that story.

How can I tell a story about our company and product, given the short attention span of our audience? Thirty seconds is enough time to tell a captivating tale that inspires a wide audience and appeals to all constituents whether motivated by logic or emotion. Those constituents will then spread the message far and fast by way of Twitter, text, Instagram, Facebook, Pinterest, e-mail, and a host of other social network methods. A gripping story is contagious and it is the most powerful branding, marketing, and sales tool available.

A number of well-known speakers, authors, academics, and practitioners are spreading the gospel of good storytelling and the critical role it plays in the success of your business. I will introduce you to just a few, share a recent example of two popular commercial storytelling examples, and provide some tips for knowing your audience. We will apply the lens of the Whole Brain Storytelling model to show how these stories are passed on and how that narration from your customers, suppliers, and employees becomes your story—the story that inspires your customers, employees, and suppliers to want to be a part of your "tribe."

There is ample research to suggest that your stakeholders are not likely to be attracted to the same message. They think, act, and are motivated differently according to different styles. Experts agree that preferences develop as a result of a combination of both nature and nurture. The degree to which we lean one way or another is the subject of ongoing debate that spans hundreds of years. The genetic predisposition we are each born with represents the nature aspect of who we are. The brain does not exist in a vacuum. Every interaction we have with the world builds our brains throughout the course of our lives. Our parents, schooling, work, and hobbies all have an impact.

Research on the brain leads us to an understanding that every individual has a preferred way and mode of thinking that affects the way we take in and process information. The awareness of one's own thinking style and the thinking styles of others, combined with the ability to act outside of one's preferred thinking style is known as "Whole Brain Thinking."

A simple model developed by Ned Herrmann in 1978, while he was the head of management development at General Electric, captures these thinking preferences. Using brain research developed by others and his own studies, Herrmann discovered that there are four patterns that emerge in terms of how the brain perceives and processes [Ref. 51] information. The Whole Brain Model emerged as a validated metaphor for describing the four different preference modes. The metaphor divides the brain into four separate quadrants. Each quadrant is different and of equal importance, as shown in the diagram following.

- The Upper Left Blue A Quadrant specializes in logical, analytical, quantitative, fact-based thinking.
- The Lower Left Green B Quadrant focuses on details and specializes in planning, organizing, and sequencing information.
- The Lower Right Red C Quadrant places a priority on feelings and the interpersonal, emotional, and kinesthetic aspects of a situation.
- The Upper Right Yellow D Quadrant synthesizes and integrates information, and is more intuitive and holistic in its thinking.

4-Quadrant Brain Model

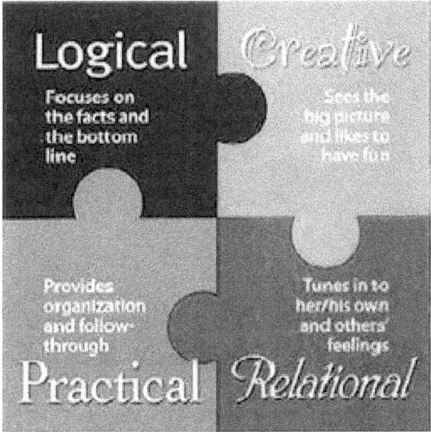

Figure 1[Ref. 52]

Due to the enormous impact of our environment throughout the course of our lives, Herrmann's theory is that we are who we are from at least 70 percent nurture and likely only 30 percent nature. Ned Herrmann developed a test called the HBDI (Herrmann Brain Dominance Instrument) to assess where in the quadrant an individual is most likely to fall. There is an abbreviated version that you might find useful in assessing your target populations. [Ref. 52]

Short of a formal assessment, there might be observable indicators you can find useful simply by walking into someone's office. If you can walk into an office and everything is in order, there is not much color to it, all the chairs are in line, all the pencils are in line, there is evidence of graphs and data, you're likely dealing with a left-brained person. Left-brained people want to be led logically through, point-by-point, the selling process.

If you go into an office and it is colorful, there are papers all over, and toys on the table, and the person stands up, comes around from behind the desk, shakes your hand, and want to talk about the weather or his or her family, you're probably dealing with a right-brain individual. That type of person is not going to be lead through a selling process. You'll have to give right-brained people one or two bullet points and let them play with it.

Regardless of individual thinking preferences, one thing is certain: a compelling story will capture everyone's interest.

Dave Kerpen, a CEO and frequent writer about entrepreneurship, summed up the importance of stories in an *Inc.* on-line magazine article published in January 2014. In it he wrote about "telling not selling." Everyone loves a good story and storytelling is a critical but often overlooked skill every business owner should have. It's not about the product, it's about how it makes people feel and stories engender feelings. Nobody likes being hit on for a sale, but everyone loves a good story. Because everybody loves a good story, if you want to sell your product to customers, your vision to investors, or your ideas to the world, you must recognize the power and importance of great storytelling [Ref. 53].

Gary Vaynerchuk is a best-selling author and speaks frequently on the importance of constructing and distributing your story content using tailor-made strategies to specific audiences on specific social media platforms. Vaynerchuk contends that while communication is still key, context matters more than ever. It's not just about developing high-quality content, but developing high-quality content perfectly adapted to specific social media platforms and mobile devices—content tailor-made for Facebook, Instagram, Pinterest, Twitter, and Tumblr. In his most recent book he uses boxing as the metaphor for putting together the combination that leads to a winning marketing strategy. [Ref. 54] He says companies committed to jabbing—patiently engaging with customers to build the relationships crucial to successful social media campaigns—want to land the "punch" that will take down their opponent or their customer's resistance in one blow. "Right hooks" convert traffic to sales and easily show results. He says a perfect right hook in today's technological world includes three characteristics: they are simple and easy to understand; they are crafted for mobile, as well as all digital devices; and they respect the nuances of the social network for which the content is intended. It is all about the right story for the right audience delivered by the right means.

Robert McKee is an award-winning writer and film director, and the world's best-known and well-respected lecturer on screen writing. He professes passionately the importance of storytelling to successful businesses. McKee recognizes that CEOs sit at the head of the table or in front of the microphone and must navigate their companies through the storms of bad economies and tough competition. But, he claims, if you look your audience in the eye, lay out your scary challenges, and say, "We'll be lucky as hell if we get through this, but here's what I think we should do," they will listen to you. To get people behind you, you must tell a truthful story. [Ref. 54]

In a 2003 interview with the senior editor of *Harvard Business Review,* McKee reiterated that persuasion is the center of business activity. He introduced a practical value creation worksheet for creating stories that inspire the audience—customers. McKee suggests a five-step method for creating a compelling story: 1) Paint a mental picture of pain for customers around the problems and costs without your capability, 2) Express the costs of doing nothing, 3) Describe how the customer will actually use your solution, not just what it is, 4) Express the potential value the customer will potentially gain from your offering, 5) Ask leading context and quantitative questions based on the buyer's story. [Ref. 55]

Authentic stories are strategic tools that create a strong brand, according to one recent book that serves as a usable step-by-step manual for writing and inculcating stories into your corporate culture and brand. [Ref. 56] Storytelling touches on something familiar but contributes to new consciousness that exposes the heart and unique culture of the company, demystifying it and making it tangible and visible. In their book, Fog and his collaborators describe how corporate stories define who we are and what we stand for. Nobody is telling customers what to do or think—they have so many choices that allow them to pick the story that best fits their own identity.

We signal to the outside world through symbols—our brand tells others who we are and what we stand for. We navigate with brands. We vote with our shopping cart, we express ourselves though consumption. Consumers want products that provide them with unique experiences—discernible values must be built into the brand.

Storytelling builds a bridge between company and consumer. The brand story gradually becomes synonymous with how we define ourselves as individuals. Products become symbols we use to tell stories. A strong brand is a combination of facts and emotions. The brand represents perceived values of a company or product. Create a product that the customer can identify with, and then add value with your brand. The difference lies in the story. Humans seek stories and experiences on their quest for a meaningful life. Make a story that the customer and employees can identify with. It will create a bond between you and you customers. Tell a story about how your company makes a difference!

An internationally renowned business scholar, Venkat Ramaswamy, provides insight into the importance of co-creating value through customer experiences in a case study of Nike and the making of their joint story in anticipation of the 2006 World Cup. [Ref. 57] His premise is that customers need no longer be mere passive recipients of value propositions offered by firms. Customers are informed, connected, networked, and empowered on an unprecedented scale thanks to search engines, proliferating Internet-based interest groups, and widespread access to high-bandwidth communication and social interaction technologies. Customers have learned how to use these new tools to make their opinions and ideas heard and are involving themselves in the value creation process. Seeing opportunity in this new environment, leading firms are responding by engaging their customers in the co-creation process and creating new value. In the process, they are inventing new competencies, business practices, and we suggest stories as well.

Nike co-created value with customers by continuously interacting with them through engagement platforms centered on customer experiences. During the 2006 World Cup, in partnership with Google, Nike set up a social networking site, Joga.com, that invited individuals to film their soccer skills, upload the videos that demonstrated their talent, and then had the network community comment on, rate, and share the user-generated content. The community was the judge of a winner every month.

Joga.com was, in effect, a thematic community that enabled individuals to share personal and collective soccer experiences. With more than one million fans participating in this innovative brand-building effort, Nike had a unique opportunity to learn directly from its customers. Nike also sponsored street soccer competitions, created a web site that connected professional players with their fans, and sponsored conventional Internet marketing programs.

Interactions like these strengthen a firm's capacity to use global network resources and thematic communities to continuously identify and act upon new innovation and value creation opportunities. By engaging with informed, connected, and networked customers around the globe, the shoe company found a new source of value. Whether as individuals or as members of communities, customers and other stakeholders can be and want to be involved in shaping outcomes of value. They do this by sharing their interactions and experiences ranging from ideas about how to improve or customize products to their feelings when using products. Through his study of Nike Dr. Ramaswamy demonstrates the power of co-creation and gives us ideas on how to design a genuinely interesting story.

Subaru recently produced an incredible storytelling commercial that appeals to both the emotional and intellectual aspects of the audience. It elicits a sentimental bond with the brand for some, and it highlights Subaru's focus on engineering and safety for others, capturing the interest of many car owners and shoppers. It last only thirty seconds and is memorable to just about anyone who sees it. If you haven't watched it, I suggest you do so at the following link: www.subaru.com/why-subaru/articles/they-lived-.html.

The story goes like this: A police officer walks up to a tow truck operator loading a horribly mangled car onto his flatbed truck. The highway patrolman says, "They lived." The tow truck driver then brings the car to the salvage yard and, when entering, tells the man at the gate, "They lived." The man who was at the gate is then talking to a colleague watching the car being off loaded and tells him the news, "They lived." The scene then cuts to the family of four who was in that car crash running to get into their new Subaru.

The family gets in their new car as the dad thinks, "We lived, thanks to our Subaru." The narrator comes in "Love. It's what makes a Subaru a Subaru." It was a short and powerful message that received mostly positive on-line reviews and inspired many to share their own Subaru stories and others to declare that their next car will be a Subaru. This is a great example of online co-creation.

Consider another recent commercial sponsored by Budweiser as part of its Super Bowl ad campaign series involving puppies and Clydesdales. It was certainly popular, and it successfully appealed to viewers' emotions. It did not introduce a rational argument for buying beer, or support the sponsor in any endeavor. This ad ran for one minute. If you haven't seen this advertisement, the link is www.budweiser.com/our-ads.html.

The story unfolds as follows: A puppy adopted by a horse rancher sets off on an adventure and gets hopelessly lost. The puppy is making his way through the rain and dark to find his way home, when he suddenly finds himself face to face with a wolf. The Clydesdales sense the puppy is in trouble and break free from the stable to rescue their little friend. The wolf gets scared off, and the horses escort the puppy back home.

The storyline lacked an element that might appeal to more logically oriented viewers but was certainly entertaining and plucked the heartstrings of many. Did it effectively communicate to beer drinkers that they should buy Budweiser? Is this genuine? It seems intended to give the impression of co-creating something with people who look like its target demographic. But it is not genuine. It is the television commercial equivalent of saccharine—it somewhat gets there, but just tastes false.

The story matters. You must understand your audience—how they think, how they communicate, and how they can help co-create a compelling image that engenders brand loyalty. The on-line environment provides a variety of means to shape and disseminate your story in concert with the very customers you hope to inspire. Value creation in the twenty-first century requires you to not only tell an interesting story, but to construct it together with employees, customers, and partners.

Recommended Reading:

Storytelling—Branding in Practice by Klaus Fog, Christian Budtz, and Baris Yakaboylu provides simple guidelines and practical tools. The book aims to inspire companies to use storytelling as a means of building their brand, internally as well as externally.

In *Storytelling in Business,* Janis Forman delivers a research-driven framework for engaging in organizational storytelling using cases from Chevron, FedEx, Phillips, and Schering-Plough. She explores how organizations can make use of storytelling to make sense of strategy, communicate it effectively, and develop or strengthen culture and brand.

We suggest Dave Kerpen's recent book, *Likeable Social Media,* for a simple, clear, and fun look about the importance of building and reinforcing your brand through social media.

We also recommend *Jab, Jab, Jab, Right Hook* by Gary Vaynerchuk as a blueprint to designing your story differently for specific social media platforms.

Chapter 8
Making the Transparency work—Glass Website
with Andrew Jacobs

The Emperor and the Seed

The emperor was growing old and he knew it was time to choose his successor. Instead of choosing one of his assistants or his children, he decided something different. He called young people in the kingdom together one day and said, "It is time for me to step down and choose the next emperor. I have decided to choose one of you."

The youth were shocked! But the emperor continued. "I am going to give each one of you a seed today—one very special seed. I want you to plant the seed, water it, and come back here after one year from today with what you have grown from this one seed. I will then judge the plants that you bring, and the one I choose will be the next emperor!"

One boy named Alexander was there that day and he, like the others, received a seed. He went home and excitedly told his mother the story. She helped him get a pot and planting soil, and he planted the seed and watered it carefully. Every day he would water it and watch to see if it had grown. After about three weeks, some of the other youth began to talk about their seeds and the plants that were beginning to grow. Alexander kept checking his seed, but nothing ever grew. Weeks went by. Still nothing. By now, others were talking about their plants but Alexander didn't have a plant, and he felt like a failure. Six months went by, still nothing in Alexander's pot. He just knew he had killed his seed.

Everyone else had trees and tall plants, but he had nothing. Alexander didn't say anything to his friends, however. He just kept waiting for his seed to grow.

A year finally went by and the youth brought their plants to the emperor for inspection. Alexander told his mother that he wasn't going to take an empty pot. But his mother told him to be honest about what happened. Alexander felt sick to his stomach, but he knew his mother was right. He took his empty pot to the palace. When Alexander arrived, he was amazed at the variety of plants grown by the others. They were beautiful in all shapes and sizes.

Alexander put his empty pot on the floor and was laughed at. A few felt sorry for him and remarked, "Nice try."

When the emperor arrived, he surveyed the room and greeted the young people. Alexander just tried to hide in the back.

"What great plants, trees and flowers you have grown," said the emperor. "Today, one of you will be appointed the next emperor!"

All of a sudden, the emperor spotted Alexander at the back of the room with his empty pot. He ordered his guards to bring him to the front. Alexander was terrified. "The emperor knows I'm a failure!" he thought. "Maybe he will have me killed!"

When Alexander got to the front, the Emperor asked him his name. "My name is Alexander," he replied.

Everyone else was laughing and making fun of him. The emperor asked for everyone's attention.

He looked at Alexander, and then announced to the crowd, "Behold your new emperor! His name is Alexander!" Alexander couldn't believe it. Alexander couldn't even grow his seed. How could he be the new emperor?

Then the emperor said, "One year ago today, I gave everyone here a seed. I told you to take the seed, plant it, water it, and bring it back to me today. But I gave you all boiled seeds, which would not grow. All of you, except Alexander, have brought me trees and plants and flowers. When you found that the seed would not grow, you substituted another seed for the one I gave you. Alexander was the only one with the courage and honesty to bring me a pot with my seed in it. Therefore, he is the one who will be the new emperor!"

—From Aesop's Fables

Alexander learned that if you plant goodness, you will reap friends. If you plant humility, you will reap greatness. If you plant perseverance, you will reap victory. If you plant consideration, you will reap harmony. If you plant hard work, you will reap success. If you plant forgiveness, you will reap reconciliation. If you plant openness, you will reap intimacy. If you plant patience, you will reap improvements. If you plant faith, you will reap miracles. Most importantly, if you plant honesty, you will reap trust—trust that builds profitability in new and exciting ways.

Throughout this book the authors have presented information, around building trusted relationships in a transparent world with customers, suppliers, and employees. If you are honest and forthright with your information and communications, you will succeed. Your brand, products, and services are no longer what you say, but what your suppliers, customers, and employees say about you and your company. The message is no longer controlled; it is posted on sites like Glass Door, LinkedIn, Twitter, Yelp, Facebook and Google.

In this chapter I will outline the steps to create a communication strategy on the web that allows a company and an individual to harness the disruptive power of transparency.

Your window to the world starts with your website or, if you are looking for a job, LinkedIn. The decision to make your communication real, authentic, and available to the rest of the world, for their use, is the measure of how successful you will be in the new, transparent world. What we found was that companies and individuals who had harnessed the power of transparency were doing two things: Individuals were creating their communication strategy using the principles from our Glass Website Diagnostic and they understood that they were not in control. They set their employees, customers, and suppliers free to tell their story.

Although it has been shown that being dishonest can result in more short-term profit, we prefer to build value over the long-term; that's what trust building through transparency can do for you. Think about it.

Think about trending, how unpredictable and random it may seem, fueled by seemingly nothing but pure emotion. Witness the rise of Justin Bieber from obscurity to international superstardom based first on a voice and good looks that mirror ten thousand other individuals who languish in obscurity, and then from consistent media coverage of an "innocent boy goes bad" storyline from which people cannot seem to tear themselves away.

Think about Justine Sacco who tweeted to her only 170 followers "Going to Africa. Hope I don't get AIDS. Just kidding. I'm white!" and, while on her eleven-hour flight, got fired and caused a worldwide firestorm of protest.

The Secret to Communicating Transparency Is . . .

The first rule of thumb in communicating transparency is to actually be real and transparent. The level of transparency is completely up to you. There are companies in the marketplace in which management has decided to publish relative salary structure within the company. Some have openly displayed pricing to its customer base. Some have invited customer participation in creation, manufacturing, distribution, marketing, order processing, quality assurance, and so on by opening up their processes to their most important constituencies. And there are companies that do *all* of these things. Conversely, many times a company does not generate trust because it does not know how to define itself. It cannot communicate its vision and values. The company or individual needs to know itself/himself in a real and meaningful way.

We have a wonderful little tool we use in the corporate identity process called the "20 Questionnaire." In it, we ask mundane questions such as what colors would be management's choices (based on color theory and emotional response, mind you; after all, we are marketing technologists) or to provide some examples of what management likes so that we can take the subjective aspect of the process and establish some "voice" to the look and feel of the logo.

We also get into some pretty hairy stuff from a self-actualization standpoint. We ask management to describe the company in one word, in one phrase, in a single statement. We ask how the phone is answered or if there is a policy around answering the phone. We ask them to describe their entire business in a single paragraph, like an elevator speech that only lasts for three floors. Invariably, after the grumbling we get some astounding responses:

"Wow, this is tough!"

"I've never thought of our company in this way."

"I can describe how I feel about the company but it may not be reality," were the responses.

In order for a company to be transparent it must to understand why it is in business, what their values are, and with whom they want to do business.

Now let's assume that you are the CEO of your company (perhaps you are) and you have developed your comfort zone in terms of transparency and can define it, what then? How do you communicate it so that it has the most impact possible? How do you create leadership and all that is brought with it? How do you construct barriers to competition? How do you developing long-lasting trust that will build upon itself. How is all this done?

How Transparency is Leveraged on the Web

First of all, let's set the record straight—in this writer's mind, the web is the single most important tool ever devised for business. Why? It is a 24/7/365 billboard for a business accessible anywhere in the world. It is totally scalable, enabling you to communicate every single aspect of your business, allowing you to communicate in different ways to customers, prospects, vendors, channel partners, influencers, regulators—you name it. In many cases the website is your business model in total, allowing utility aspects of order tracking, process tracking, billing, collecting, information dissemination, and so on to happen automatically saving untold time, money and, effort and shoring up relationships. It is magic.

But only to those who truly leverage its power, and most do not even come close. So there are many businesspeople who *hate* their websites. Their websites are a nuisance, an annoyance, something you have to have. A website is the all-powerful lens others need to harness the power of the Internet, and level the playing field with any competitor. Everyone is checking you, your products and services on the web. Our standard of behavior is to first and foremost check out a company, product, or service website as part of the vetting process, no matter where the information or lead came from. So now, one gets an impulse or hears something and immediately, the smart phone comes out, and the information starts flowing real time, right there on the spot.

Now there are some required elements when it comes to the presentation of your website. They are the underpinnings of the trust that you convey with your content.

Design: in terms of aesthetics, just like other aspects of life, there are some websites that are beautifully designed—many aspects of it just seem to fit together and some not so much. It really comes down to math. That's right, mathematics and ratios govern much of what our brains understand and judge to be good and bad. There are myriad examples in nature: if you cut a conch shell and look at a cross section you'll see that nature has formed certain exacting ratios of how the shell is formed in a circular motion. It's the same thing with music. The way that music is formed, and the way that certain sounds and notes play well together and others don't is all mathematical. Snowflakes are geometric and perfect, and each one of literally trillions is different. Some people would say that's God, and maybe it does have a little bit to do with some kind of universal intelligence, but to me it's just the right amount of certain numbers.

The human brain recognizes when math works and when math doesn't work. From a design standpoint, it's called the Golden Rule—a formula that governs the way that images, content, and words are depicted on a page and interpreted by the brain. Even a Jackson Pollack painting, as random as the paint splatter seems, has a certain order to it that is only explained through mathematical formulas such as the Golden Ratio. [Ref. 58]

The other given is the technical prowess built into a website. A website should be reviewed and probably upgraded every two years or so due to technical changes in the Internet that can affect how the site is rendered and presented. Changes in the platform on which the site was built, WordPress for example, changes in browsers such as Chrome or Internet Explorer and changes in the operating system of the computer or device used to view the site.

All of these can have cataclysmic effects on the delivery of the site. Security holes can be opened and hackers can inject your site with rogue content or use your site to spam around the world, and so on. But more than that, the way the information is presented changes dramatically from year to year. Screen resolutions as wide as 1920 or more now give companies the ability to tell their stories with broad, bold, beautiful graphics and photos. This was not available a few years ago.

Now combine these best-of-breed practices on the design and technical side with total transparency in content delivery and can you see how powerful your messaging to the marketplace can be?

The Glass Website

Here is what The Glass Website can do for you. It is a fantastic public vehicle to display your "Why?"

Why you exist in the marketplace.
Why customers should do business with you.
Why you are better than competitors.

Transparency plays a major role in that it provides the objectivity for users to believe your message. So it is not you telling the world why you exist, why customers should do business with you, or why you are better; it is your public that is doing the "evangelizing" for you. Now, you may think that soliciting reviews, comments, and so forth and posting them online is dangerous but if you start with the premise that the organization is honest about what it delivers and how it delivers, that danger is minimized. Furthermore, studies have shown that brand loyalty actually increases when a company has made a mistake in some way but makes good in a reasonable amount of time. So how much danger is there in leveraging transparency to let your constituents deliver your message? This is true co-creation with your customers, suppliers, and people in an open, flexible, imaginative, creative, fun, and spontaneous environment.

For example, an organization whose associates coach business owners shows on its website an image of a befuddled business owner with Post-It® notes placed all over his head. (http://www.thealternativeboard.com). Written on the post-its are messages such as: "do this," "do that," "make time," and so on—all typical elements of a business owner's crazy workload and lack of time. The caption reads "Look familiar?" which immediately creates a pain point and elicits an emotion from the intended target that "wow, these guys get me." A relationship is immediately created and the dynamics of the transparent Internet engage resulting in a post, a tweet, a repost or re-Tweet, a graphic pass-along on Facebook, and so on. It's probably going to happen organically so why not take advantage of the situation and actually ask for the interaction? Once it's out there, it can take on a life of its own—a pretty good thing from a single communication.

The Glass Website also allows you the opportunity to tell the truth about your company and industry on the web in this day and age setting the table for true success.

You'll never be put into a defensive position

Be consistent and you won't have to deal with the impression of impropriety. These days people can smell lies, untruths, and embellishment—it is a part of the glass society we live in.

A great example is Wild Planet Foods. On the company website (www.wildplanetfoods.com), much of the content is dedicated to explaining in detail why most fishing is done non-sustainably, and how Wild Planet differs in its practices. It explains why Wild Planet fish are so much more nutritious and how the fishing techniques actually affect this. The FAQ section is comprehensive and many of the provocative questions are actually answered in video form by Wild Planet CEO Bill Carvalho, who is one of the foremost experts in sustainable fishing in the world. He actually carries this transparency to the granular level by answering every single e-mailed or snail mailed question personally with a complete explanation. People who are at first skeptical about Wild Planet and then become advocates after being exposed to Mr. Carvalho, are called "Bill-lievers." Moreover, Wild Planet encourages reviews of their products as well as customer recipes that they prepare, photograph, and publish. The result? Some of the most loyal and fervent customers in the industry and a position as the unquestioned leader in sustainable canned fish products worldwide.

With this example of Wild Planet, you can see how The Glass Website can and will increase customer loyalty.

B2C [Ref. 59]—Through transparent information, offerings, discounts, and competitive pricing to existing customers

B2B-Through transparent display of processes throughout the life of an order and the utility value of having customers collaborate in different parts of the process. It's okay for customers to see that an order may be two days late if they have logged on and see that the trucking company has been crippled by a snowstorm.

You can properly manage expectations because The Glass Website communicates your organization's real capabilities to the market, thus attracting only those companies for whom you can add real value, thereby saving untold time and money

It increases the opportunities in the marketplace.

It conversely forces your organization to go into a public continual improvement mode in order to broaden value and customer base.

It provides for immediate comparison to competitors so the organization is forced to improve its offerings.

It can help reinforce the most critical relationships with the people who count: your customers.

Real testimonials and peer reviews (even if negative, but responded to with thoughtfulness and timeliness) are intoxicating for people looking for the truth in what they are reading.

Give-and-take dialogue with customers that give them a vested interest in the brands they are choosing and reinforce their choices.

The Glass Company Website Diagnostic

How transparent are you in your web delivery? Here is a quick six-question diagnostic that can help you determine your transparency level:

How Often Do You Change or Add Information to Your Site?
A. Every week
B. Every month
C. Once every three months
D. Once every six months
E. Once per year

Do You Allow for Reviews or Comments on Your Site and Do you Police Them?
A. I allow complete unrestrained comments.
B. I allow comments but edit them.
C. I allow comments but reserve the right to deny publishing.
D. I do not allow comments.

Are You Speaking to Your Customers' Issues or Selling Products/Services?
A. I have case studies about how we impacted our customers on my home page.
B. I have case studies in my site but not on my home page.
C. My home page content is mostly about my company or our products/services.

What is the utility level of your site?
A. I have an automated system that allows customers to see where their order sits or where we are in the work process at any time.
B. I have chat or contact number internally or furnish that information for our channel partners during business hours.
C. I do not have the facility online to check orders or cite where we are in our customer relationship.

Do You Cite the Three To Five Biggest Issues in Your Industry Online, Expound Opinions and Policy, and Invite Users to Comment?
A. We have news feeds and other sources for industry issues and opinions and offer an open forum for comments.
B. We have news feeds and other sources for industry issues but do not have a facility for comment.
C. We do not have a news and opinion section.

Answer Key

How often do you change or add information to your site?

    A. 10 points

    B. 7 Points

    C. 5 Points

    D. 3 Points

    E. 1 Point

Do you allow for reviews or comments on your site and do you police them?

    A. 10 Points

    B. 7 Points

    C. 5 Points

    D. 3 Points

Are You Speaking to Your Customers' Issues or Selling Products/Services?

    A. 10 Points

    B. 5 Points

    C. 3 Points

What is the Utility Level of Your Site?

    A. 10 Points

    B. 5 Points

    C. 1 Point

Do You Cite the Three To Five Biggest Issues in Your Industry Online, Expound Opinions and Policy and Invite Users to Comment?

    A. 10 Points

    B. 5 Points

    C. 1 Point

Do You Have an FAQ Section On Your Site?

    A. 10 Points

    B. 5 Points

    C. 1 Point

If you Scored :

- 60 points you are a king/queen of transparency and should be proud of your openness.
- 59–34 points and you are pretty transparent and ready to totally open yourself up.
- 33–22 points shows that you have good intentions but need to ratchet up the transparency.
- Less than 22 points and you probably need to shore up your business practices and once that is complete, let your customers, vendors, employees, and other significant people announce it to the world!

In closing, you probably have everything you need to project the most fantastic image and truth about your company to anyone who will listen. All you have to do is be honest and forthright in your company's culture, policies, and commitment to your public and then deliver it by way of the all powerful Worldwide Web. That's total transparency and it will work for you as nothing else you've ever experienced in business.

Final Thoughts

To harness the disruptive nature of transparency in our business, we need to accept that this truth actually provides a better solution, even if it is negative. In a transparent world a difference of opinion is not a negative but an incentive to revisit and reestablish core values, initiatives, and roles to achieve the company vision. *To be transparent is to expose our core beliefs and values for scrutiny by our stakeholders.* So why would we lift the proverbial kimono? If you do not do it, someone will do it for you.

Your story is no longer your story. Your employees, customers, and suppliers are telling your story where their comments are recorded on the Internet forever. The business world is now an open book, including the way you conduct business with your suppliers, and your costs, the salaries of your employees, as well as how you treat your employees and customers. To become transparent in your business practices allows you and your business to flourish.

Flourishing involves aligning our values and the values of our business with the values our customers and society hold dear. To *flourish* is to have more than financial success. Flourishing adds the individual and social dimensions of human well-being and the well-established concept of sustainability. At its core flourishing is a function of *connectedness* and *meaning* between people. When we focus our business on being transparent we are able to flourish

This is the disruptive nature of transparency: controlling *with* versus *controlling over* your employees, suppliers, and customers. We co-create a common vision for our company with our employees, customers and suppliers. We recognize that do well and excel, in the transparent business world, stakeholders are more than targets to bombard with messages—they are bridges for their messages and a means for broader dissemination enabled by the Internet.

About the Authors

Dr. William Paolillo

Bill Paolillo has his Doctorate of Management and is the President and Owner of The Alternative Board, Suffolk County, New York. Throughout the years, Bill has been involved in all aspects of running a business—from the tough early days of a startup right through to the sale of a successful business, helping companies go from losses to profit and dramatically grow sales and market share along the way.

Bill is a published author and national blogger. His *Ted Talk*, "Love: The Other Four Letter Word that Drives Your Business," is based upon his academic research at Case Western Reserve University. Bill believes the coolest thing you can do is share something with someone, have it make a positive impact on their business and that person's life, and he or she passes it on. "Small and medium size business is my passion," says Bill.

A native of Long Island, Bill has held a wide variety of interesting jobs, ranging from President of Sales to taxi driver. Bill has more than twenty-five years' experience as a senior executive at businesses such as Black & Decker, Procter & Gamble, ICI Paints, McGraw-Hill Construction, Homax Group in sales, marketing, and general management.

Contact Information:
wjpaolillo@gmail.com
www.linkedin.com/in/williampaolillo

Dr. David Grogan

David Grogan spends his time leading and studying transformational change in government, defense, and technology sector organizations that deliver complex information services to a wide and diverse customer set.

He specializes in the ability to quickly build new programs, and establish well-organized, highly productive teams. Focusing on people and getting them to concentrate on a common vision, deliberate strategy, and disciplined execution while remaining alert, agile, and adaptable in a dynamic environment is the key to flourishing.

As a general manager, president, and COO, David successfully led several business units and companies through the challenging period associated with mergers and acquisitions. During a twenty-year military career, he served in the infantry, military intelligence, and as an Arabic speaking Foreign Area Officer (FAO) with assignments in the 82nd Airborne Division, 3rd Infantry Division, 1st Armored Division, United Nations, and US embassies abroad. His Army experience included more than a dozen years overseas highlighted by multiple combat tours and duty throughout Europe, the Middle East, and Africa.

David's recent doctoral studies focused on designing sustainable businesses that benefit the environment, the economy, and society. His dissertation investigated improving value creation following mergers and acquisitions. His award-winning doctoral research centered on the experiences and decisions of acquired executives and other key leaders during post-merger integration.

Contact Information:

dpg24@case.edu

www.linkedin.com/pub/david-grogan/64/757/947

Dr. Edward Straub

Dr. Straub is responsible for a unique program that takes an innovative approach to robotics. Dr. Straub has led this technology transition by studying the operational and social effect of prototypes used in real-world applications. He has presented to cabinet-level executives at the White House and international audiences.

Dr. Straub's previous experience includes consultant and strategic planner for automotive, utilities, and defense clients on acquisition, supply chain management, and software system integration projects. As a Marine Corps officer, he served as the senior program manager for Buildings, Health, and Education reconstruction projects in Baghdad, Iraq, and earlier as a combat engineer company commander in Ar Ramadi, Iraq.

Dr. Straub earned his Bachelor of Science in Geology in 1994 and his Master of Business Administration in 2002. His doctoral research, completed in 2015 at Case Western Reserve University, focused on team dynamics. Dr. Straub's research uncovered interesting parallels between factors contributing to healthy family functioning and work teams operating in small world network environments.

A self-described serial learner, Dr. Straub's other educational experiences include: Certified SAP Consultant from the SAP Academy (2002); Project Management Professional from the Project Management Institute (2009); and Master's Certificate, IS/IT Project Management from Villanova University (2009).

Contact Information:

edwstraub@gmail.com

www.linkedin.com/profile/view?id=26601717

Joe Mazzella

Joe Mazzella is a sales, business development, and process leader with multi-discipline industry expertise and a more than twenty-year track record of success in growing revenues and profits. Joe is a Six Sigma Black Belt productivity specialist, developing, implementing, and measuring strategies. His systematic approach utilizes key metrics for reporting, analyzing data, and measuring results. Joe is passionate about the creation and effective use of technology to enhance business processes, strategy, planning, and execution, utilizing design and implementation of sales communications and training initiatives, lead generation programs, sales targets, and compensation models.

Joe Mazzella's past work experience includes leadership roles with McGraw-Hill Construction and Akzo Nobel. Job responsibilities have included publisher, vice president of transactional sales, director of sales operations, Lean Six Sigma Black Belt, and business process leader. Joe is currently Vice President and Partner of 3fitt, Inc. where he is responsible for sales, marketing, and general business processes for integrated Wellness Platform, utilizing outcome-based programming to motivate individuals to take charge of their health and help companies improve the health of their employees resulting in increased productivity, lower healthcare costs, revenue growth, and the overall wellness of the organization, 3fitt, Inc.

Contact Information:

jmazzella@engineeringdirector.com
www.linkedin.com/in/joemazzella/en

Chuck Sarka

Chuck Sarka is an organizational anthropologist and leadership coach specializing in strategic human resources, change management, team building, positive employee relations, and leadership development. He has spent the last thirty-eight years studying group dynamics that foster positive relations between leadership teams and their followers. Chuck has worked developing positive work environments and building leadership teams across the globe including, South America, Mexico, China, Singapore, Indonesia, Philippines, Hong Kong, Australia, Canada, and the UK.

Chuck graduated from Heidelberg College with concentrations in both economics and psychology and then went on to obtain a master's degree from Cleveland State University. He is certified in many of the top assessment tools, which he blends together help from high performance heterogeneous thinking groups as well to set the stage for individual career counseling and job enrichment.

Chuck's high-energy "Thought-ta-tional"™ speaking style has been used by Delta, Wells Fargo, Hoover-Dirt Devil, USIS, Phoenix Steel, Homax, Welty Construction, Stanly Black and Decker, and GE to revive and transform leadership principles into everyday practices that build on the fact that "The size Bite you get out of Life is based on the IMPACT that you make" and that there is an "I" in team, leading to bottom-line productivity.

Contact Information:

csarka@me.com
www.linkedin.com/in/chucksarka

Dr. Solange Charas, PhD

Solange Charas is CEO of Charas Consulting, providing advisory services to boardsand C-suite executives, optimizing return on human capital investment from individuals, teams, and organization-wide programs. She is a recognized expert in human resources (HR) analytics, specializing in mergers and acquisitions transactions. She serves on the boards of Able Energy (NASDAQ) and Integral Board Group where she is their chief human resources officer (CHRO). Solange is an adjunct professor in the master's program at NYU.

Solange has deep experience in all areas of HR, specializing in human capital metrics, using proprietary evidence-based tools. These analytical approaches allow organizations to improve corporate leadership effectiveness, employee productivity, and merger and acquisition (M&A) success. She has participated in more than fifty M&A transactions. Dr. Charas' doctorate research focused on innovative approaches to select, develop, and manage passionate, high-performing interdisciplinary teams at the Board and C-suite level, and resulted in quantifying executive team effect on corporate financial performance. She is a certified Team Coach.

Prior to receiving her PhD, Solange was the CHRO at Praetorian Financial Services Group (acquired by QBE), the SVP HR at Benfield (acquired by Aon), and the CHRO at EuroRSCG, the largest division of Havas Advertising. In her client-serving endeavors she held various senior level positions at Arthur Andersen, Ernst & Young, Towers Watson, and GE Capital, providing board and C-suite advisory services.

Dr. Charas has a BA from UC Berkeley, an MBA from Cornell University, and a PhD in Management from Case Western Reserve University. She has been published in various professional and academic venues including Harvard *Business Review, The Conference Board's Director Notes, Entrepreneur* magazine, *The Corporate Board Magazine, Fortune* magazine, *Chief Executive* magazine, *The Chicago Tribune, Fast Company* magazine, and the *International Journal of Disclosure and Governance.* She has appeared on various business media, including *Bloomberg for Small Business, NACD Board Vision,* and CNN's *iReport.*

Contact Information:

sc@charasconsulting.com

www.linkedin.com/pub/dr-solange-charas/0/9a0/375

Andy Jacobs

Andy Jacobs is Managing Director of Marketecture Group, a Didit Company. Didit is a leading digital marketing agency and the originator of paid search. Today Marketecture Group acts as the strategic consultancy for Didit prospects and clients, enabling a comprehensive end-to-end marketing solution including strategic, creative, production and traditional/e-marketing outreach. With positioning around "Building Brands, Constructing Opportunities," this new venture grew out of the need to provide the same best-in-class strategic guidance and targeted creative communications excellence afforded to larger organizations with significant budgets to small and mid-marketplace companies with less capital resources.

With a rich, thirty-five-year heritage working with more than a thousand B2B and B2C entities from divisions of Fortune 500 companies to funded start-ups, in every industry possible within a broad range of trade classes, Andy's "Strategy First" mantra provides for optimal ROI for his clients. Andy holds degrees in Communications and Marketing from the State University of New York and has taken continuing education and certificate courses in Marketing with the School of Visual Arts, Harvard Business School, Yale Business School, Stamford, and Columbia University. He has been active in civic and professional organizations, including the Make-A-Wish Foundation, Business Information Group, the Leukemia and Lymphoma Society, the Long Island Philharmonic, the Long Island Advertising Club, the Pat Covelli Foundation, and other organizations, serving on their executive boards. Andy is an ongoing contributor to several marketing blogs providing thought leadership and practical advice. He is also an avid triathlete having completed two Ironman races. Andy now serves USA Triathlon, the Children's Tumor Foundation, and the Leukemia and Lymphoma Society as a Certified Coach. He is married, has two grown children and resides in Huntington, New York.

Contact Information:

Andrew.Jacobs@linx.com

www.linkedin.com/in/marketingologist

Debra Mazzella

Deb Mazzella's mantra throughout her career has been, and continues to be, "empowerment through education." From working in the proverbial trenches, to marketing roles at regional and national levels, as well as collaborating with business owners and senior management as a consultant, Deb brings creative solutions focused on business, professional, and personal growth.

Contact Information:
dmazzella@v4u.nu
www.linkedin.com/in/debramazzella

References

1. For a thorough treatment on sustainability and how a flourishing business can do well by doing good, we recommend, Embedded Sustainability: The Next Big Competitive Advantage, by Laszlo and Zhexembayeva (2011) and The Flourishing Enterprise: The New Spirit of Business by Laszlo and Brown (2014).

2. Http://www.globescan.com/component/edocman/?view=document&id=17 1&Itemid=591

3. http://www.reinventingorganizations.com

4. C. Laszlo and J. S. Brown, *Flourishing Enterprise: The New Spirit of Business.* Stanford, CA: Stanford Business Press, 2014.

5. R. M. Ryan and E. L. Deci, "Intrinsic and Extrinsic Motivations: Classic Definitions and New Directions," *Contemp. Educ. Psychol.*, vol. 25, no. 1, pp. 54–67, Jan. 2000.

6. http://jom.sagepub.com/content/34/3/410

7. S. I. Tannenbaum, J. E. Mathieu, and D. Cohen, "Teams Are Changing: Are Research and Practice Evolving Fast Enough?," *Ind. Organ. Psychol.*, vol. 5, pp. 2–24, 2012.

8. G. A. Neuman and J. Wright, "Team Effectiveness: Beyond Skills and Cognitive Ability," *J. Appl. Psychol.*, vol. 84, no. 3, pp. 376–89, Jun. 1999.

9. D. Goleman, *Social Intelligence: The New Science of Human Relationships.* New York: Bantam Dell, 2006.

10. D. Goleman, R. Boyatzis, and A. McKee, "The Hidden Driver of Great Performance," *Harvard Business Review*, pp. 1–11, Dec-2001.

11. V. Urch Druskat and S. B. Wolff, "Building the Emotional Intelligence of Groups," *Harvard Business Review*, pp. 80–09, Mar-2001.

12. R. Gilkey, R. Caceda, and C. Kilts, "When Emotional Reasoning Trumps IQ," *Harvard Business Review*, p. 1, Sep-2010.

13. D. Goleman, *Working With Emotional Intelligence.* Random House Publishing Group, 2006. p.317.

14. D. Goleman, *Emotional Intelligence*, vol. 10th Anniv. New York: Bantam Dell, 2005.

15. V. U. Druskat and S. B. Wolff, "Building the emotional intelligence of groups," *Harv. Bus. Rev.*, vol. 79, no. 3, pp. 80–90, 164, Mar. 2001.

16. http://pubsonline.informs.org/doi/abs/10.1287/orsc.1050.0133

17. J. L. Carlo, K. Lyytinen, and R. J. Boland, "Dialectics of Collective Minding: Contradictory Appropriations of Information Technology in a High-Risk Project," *MIS Q.*, vol. 36, no. 4, pp. 1081–1108, 2012.

18. http://jmi.sagepub.com/cgi/doi/10.1177/1056492606291202

19. W. B. Schaufeli, M. Salanova, V. Gonzalez-Roma, and A. B. Bakker, "The Measurement of Engagement and Burnout: A Two Sample Confirmatory Factor Analytic Approach," *J. Happiness Stud.*, vol. 3, pp. 71–92, 2002.

20. http://doi.apa.org/getdoi.cfm?doi=10.1037/0021-9010.88.3.518

21. http://businessjournal.gallup.com/content/247/the-high-cost-of-disengaged-employees.aspx.

22. http://businessjournal.gallup.com/content/162953/tackle-employees-stagnating-engagement.aspx.

23. http://amj.aom.org/content/49/1/49

24. http://www.jstor.org/stable/10.2307/2776392 p. 1364

25. http://asq.sagepub.com/content/44/1/82

26. http://www.emeraldinsight.com/doi/abs/10.110

27. http://journal.frontiersin.org/article/10.3389/fpsyg.2014.01335

28. http://www.emeraldinsight.com/10.1108/02621710610678445

29. http://hum.sagepub.com/cgi/doi/10.1177/001872679905200201

30. http://www.jstor.org/stable/2667088

31. http://psycnet.apa.org/index.cfm?fa=search.displayRecord&uid=2004-00226-001

32. http://doi.apa.org/getdoi.cfm?doi=10.1037/0003-066X.45.2.120

33. B. Olson, W. Paolillo, and E. Straub, "The Big Industry that Couldn't: Flourishing in Modern Design & Construction," Case Western Reserve University, 2015."

34. Bureau of Labor Statistics (BLS) data

35. Zika-Viktorsson, Sundström, & Engwall, 2006

36. BLS data

37. Unpublished study, Saville Consulting

38. BLS data, http://www.marketwatch.com/story/the-looming-us-labor-shortage-2012-03-14

39. http://jom.sagepub.com/content/40/3/820.short

40. https://hbr.org/product/what-makes-a-team-smarter-more-women/an/F1106D-PDF-ENG

41. http://www.fastcompany.com/3036365/strong-female-lead/a-mathematical-approach-to-appointing-more-women-to-your-board

42. Stigler, G. J. (1961). The Economics of Information. *Journal of Political Economy, 69*(3), 213-225.

43. http://press.princeton.edu/titles/10493.html

44. http://library.fora.tv/2008/02/05/Joseph_Stiglitz_Economics_of_Informati on

45. http://books.google.com/books?id=B-qxrPaU1-MC&printsec=frontcover#v=onepage&q&f=false

46. Nonaka, I., von Krogh, G.,and Voelpel, S. 2006. "Organizational Knowledge Creation Theory: Evolutionary Paths and Future Advances," *Organization Studies*, 27(8): 1179–1208.

47. https://hbr.org/2004/10/cultural-intelligence/ar/1

48. As a PhD, all my work includes that of those who have come before me and my research is a collaboration of advisors and others.

49. Captured in an interview conducted by Ariel Schwartz with Blake Mycoskie for Fast Company.com posted on September 6, 2011. http://www.fastcompany.com/1776334/toms-shoes-ceo-blake-mycoskie-social-entrepreneurship-telling-stories-and-his-new-book (accessed on 5/24/2015)

50. Captured in an interview conducted by Rich Brooks with Gary Vaynerchuk for Fast Company.com posted on October 12, 2009.http://www.fastcompany.com/1401023/how-cash-your-passion-interview-gary-vaynerchuk (accessed on 5/24/2011).

51. http://www.herrmannsolutions.com/ (accessed on 5/24/2015).The Whole Brain Model and four color 4-quadrant graphic are trademarks for Herrmann International. © 2012.

52. Access this link for further information. The diagnostic instrument is available at Herrmann International: http://www.herrmannsolutions.com/.

53. Kerpen, D. (January 17, 2014). INC.com. Retrieved from INC.com. "13 Quotes to Inspire Your Inner Storyteller": http://www.inc.com/dave-kerpen/you-need-to-become-a-better-storyteller-heres-some-inspiration.html (accessed on 5/24/2015).

54. Vaynerchuk, G. (2013). *Jab, Jab, Jab, Right Hook: How to Tell Your Story in a Noisy Social World.* Harper Business.

55. McKee, R. &. (2003). "Storytelling that moves people," Harvard Business Review, 51–55.

56. Ibid.

57. Fog, K., Budtz, C., Munch, P., & Blanchette, S. (2011). *Storytelling: Branding in Practice.* Springer Science & Business Media.

58. In mathematics, two quantities are in the golden ratio if their ratio is the same as the ratio of their sum to the larger of the two quantities. (See "Golden Ratio" in the Wikipedia.)

59. Business to Consumer (B2C).